THE MODI MYTH

S. NIHAL SINGH

PARANJOY

First published in India in 2015 by Paranjoy Guha Thakurta
paranjoy@gmail.com

Copyright © S. Nihal Singh 2015
ISBN: 9789384439576

Surendra Nihal Singh asserts the moral right to be identified as the
author of this work.

First Edition

Typeset in 11/15 Adobe Garamond Pro by Ram Das Lal, NCR Delhi

Cover design: PealiDezine

Publishing facilitation: AuthorsUpFront

Dedication

To those who aspire for a better India

CONTENTS

PUBLISHER'S NOTE

Surendra Nihal Singh is more than one of India's seniormost journalists, having edited three prestigious daily newspapers. He is one of the country's most respected commentators on the state of the polity. In this book, which he describes as akin to a long essay, he situates Prime Minister Narendra Modi against the wider canvas of contemporary Indian politics. Analysing his tenure at the end of fifteen months, he effectively argues that Modi can never hope to become an 'inclusive' and widely accepted head of the government of the world's largest democracy unless he jettisons the narrow vision of India that is propagated by the Rashtriya Swayamsevak Sangh (RSS) which is considered to be the ideological parent of the Bharatiya Janata Party (BJP).

The question that is raised in the book is whether the BJP under Modi, which has for the first time in three decades won a majority of seats in the Lok Sabha in 2014, can hope to break away from the RSS, at least on specific issues relating to preserving the inclusive character of Indian society. The tussle between the Nehruvian idea of India and the notion of a Hindu Rashtra propagated by the RSS is the defining *leitmotif* of the current regime in New Delhi. It is this recurring theme that finds expression in Nihal Singh's book—that flits across time, space, parties and personalities—to contextualize present-day politics in India against an expansive backdrop of people and places.

In the three years between 2013 and 2015, hardly a month has gone when a new book on Modi has not been published. Many of these are unabashed hagiographies with no pretence to objectivity. This book, on the other hand, is not just a balanced account but seeks to take a close and critical look at Modi, not just the person but the politician, the demagogue and the administrator as well. He compares and contrasts Modi with his predecessors, including Atal Behari Vajpayee. Written in a racy style, Nihal Singh straddles the world of contemporary political history of India with consummate ease.

It is my honour and privilege to publish this book as the first under a new imprint. I am grateful to my colleagues Jyotirmoy Chaudhuri and Maya Palit for the pains they took over finalizing the book and to Shachi Seth and Ajita Banerjie as well for reading the manuscript. I look forward to publishing 86-year-old Nihal Singh's second novel, which promises more than its share of excitement and titillation.

Paranjoy Guha Thakurta
October 2015

PREFACE

I would like to consider this a long essay rather than a conventional book. What impelled me to write it is that the Narendra Modi phenomenon represents a break from the more than six-decades-long political philosophy of independent India.

True, the Bharatiya Janata Party (BJP) had governed the country for six years under Atal Behari Vajpayee in a coalition government. Although Vajpayee was a BJP member and proclaimed his allegiance to the party's ideological mentor, the 'social organization' Rashtriya Swayamsevak Sangh (RSS), he continued to rule in the Nehruvian tradition of India's first prime minister, Jawaharlal Nehru, while tolerating the packing of official and semi-official organizations with RSS men and women. In short, Vajpayee was an inclusive leader, relying on his poetic gifts to reconcile glaring contradictions in his approach.

Modi, India's current prime minister, is cast in another mould, stronger in his loyalty to the RSS, an organization in which he was nurtured, more combative and more ambitious with a greater awareness of the potential of modern technology. His ideal, outside of his RSS mentors, is Sardar Vallabhbhai Patel, India's first home minister, rather than Nehru, and he is a believer in the philosophy of Hindutva and all that it stands for.

It was his good fortune that his national political advent came after the disappointing tenure of the United Progressive Alliance coalition between 2004 and 2014, which lost steam in its last three years, and was hobbled by a series of scams. He was, of course, trading on his more than twelve-year-long record as Gujarat's chief minister as an able, no-nonsense administrator. But his ambition is not merely to develop the country as a prosperous modern state but also to change the character and moorings that have underpinned India in a decidedly Hindu direction. Reconciling the contradictions involved in this exercise will be his formidable task in a nation of many faiths, languages and outlooks.

I have dipped into my political columns (courtesy *The Asian Age* and *The Tribune*) to buttress my arguments.

GUJARAT'S SHADOW

To those who interacted with him during his days as a functionary of the Bharatiya Janata Party (BJP) at its headquarters in New Delhi, Narendra Modi stood out distinctly. While his colleagues would on occasion jest at their own or their party's expense, he would never let down his guard.

India and the world are now familiar with the man of humble origin, married off at a young age, who left his wife and home to seek something different. He was attracted to the BJP's ideological mentor, the Rashtriya Swayamsevak Sangh (RSS), perhaps by its no-nonsense approach to life. After sowing his version of wild oats by meditating in the hills, among other activities, he joined the RSS family in earnest.

But behind the mask of the avid worker imbibing the RSS's truths with their high quotient of myths and fantasies, he was weaving his way into the higher reaches of the organization. He was a good worker, fulfilling the tasks allotted to him with diligence, including a stretch of the BJP's veteran leader Lal Krishna Advani's *rath yatra* (chariot pilgrimage), in the cause of building a temple to replace the sixteenth-century Babri Masjid at Ayodhya in Uttar Pradesh.

Modi's big moment came when political circumstances in his

native Gujarat led to the need to install a new BJP leader as chief minister. But even as he set about demonstrating his acumen in governance and getting the better of his political foes within the RSS, the BJP and outside, came the tragedy of the 2002 anti-Muslim riots. More than 1,000 Muslims were killed. The cause was the mysterious torching of train wagons of BJP supporters returning from the Ayodhya pilgrimage, which provoked an immediate response.

The Gujarat administration led by Modi was, on the face of it, derelict in its duties, acting only after many lives were lost, women raped, homes torched, and countless avoidable tragedies had occurred. Court proceedings did lead to convictions, including that of a junior minister in Modi's cabinet. Modi has never acknowledged his culpability, if only in delaying action, because he realizes it would be the thin end of the wedge.

Years later he tried to explain himself in an interview to Reuters news agency in July 2013, only to come to grief. He said in part:

Narendra Modi: Another thing, any person if we are driving a car, we are a driver, and someone else is driving a car and we're sitting behind, even then if a puppy comes under the wheel, will it be painful or not? Of course it is. If I'm a chief minister or not, I'm a human being. If something bad happens anywhere, it is natural to be sad.

Q: Do you believe India should have a secular leader?

Modi: We do believe that ... But what is the definition of secularism? For me, my secularism is, India first. I say, the philosophy of my party is 'Justice to all. Appeasement to none.' This is our secularism.

In relation to the 2002 Gujarat riots, in a television interview to Karan Thapar on CNN-IBN in October 2007, he thought it wiser to end the interaction abruptly, than to answer tough questions. Here is an excerpt from the interview:

Karan Thapar: Mr Narendra Modi, let's start by talking about you. In the six years that you have been the chief minister of Gujarat, the Rajiv Gandhi Foundation has declared Gujarat to be the best administered state. *India Today*, on two separate occasions, declared that you are the most efficient chief minister and despite that people still call you, to your face, a mass murderer. And they accuse you of being prejudiced against Muslims. Do you have an image problem?

Narendra Modi: I think it's not proper to say that (there are) people. There are two or three persons who talk in this terminology and I always say God bless them.

Thapar: You are saying this is the conspiracy of two or three persons only.

Modi: I have not said so.

Thapar: But you are saying its only two or three people.

Modi: This is the information I have. It's the people's voice.

Thapar: Can I point out to you that in September 2003 the Supreme Court said that they had lost faith in the Gujarat government. In April 2004 the Chief Justice of the Supreme Court said that you were like a modern day Nero who looks the other side when helpless children and innocent women are burned. The Supreme Court seems to have a problem with you.

Modi: Karan, I have a small request to make. Please go through the SC judgment. If there is anything in writing, I'll be happy to know everything.

Thapar: There was nothing in writing, you are right. It was an observation.

Modi: If it is in (the) judgment then I'll be happy to give you the answer.

Thapar: But do you mean a criticism by the Chief Justice in court doesn't matter?

Modi: It's a simple request. Please go through the court judgment. Hand out the sentence you are quoting and let the people know it.

Thapar: OK. It wasn't just an open comment made by the Chief Justice. In August 2004, the Supreme Court reopened 2,100 cases out of a total of 4,600—almost 40 per cent—and they did so because they believed that justice hadn't happened in Gujarat.

Modi: I'll be happy. Ultimately the court of law will take the judgment.

Thapar: But isn't this the reason that despite the fact *India Today* called you the best chief minister, Rajiv Gandhi Foundation said Gujarat is the best administered state, people say Modi is prejudiced against the Muslims. This is why I ask you, do you have an image problem?

Modi: Actually, I have not spent a single minute on my image and that can also be a reason. I am busy with my work. I am committed to Gujarat. I am dedicated to Gujarat. I never talk about my image. I never spent a single minute for my image and therefore confusions may be there.

Thapar: I'll tell you what the problem is. Even five years after the Gujarat killings of 2002 the ghost of Gujarat still haunts you. Why have you not done more to allay that ghost?

Modi: This I gave it to the media persons like Karan Thapar. Let them enjoy.

Thapar: Can I suggest something to you?

Modi: I have no problem.

Thapar: Why can't you say that you regret the killings that happened? Why can't you say may be the government should have done more to protect them?

Modi: What I had to say I have said at that time and you can find out my statements.

Thapar: Just say it again.

Modi: Not necessary I have to talk about in 2007 everything you want to talk about.

Thapar: But by not saying it again, by not letting people hear the message repeatedly you are allowing an image contrary to Gujarat to continue. It's in your hands to change it.

Modi: (*Takes the microphone off.*) I'll have to rest. I need some water.

Thapar: *Pani* (Water).

Modi: *Dosti bani rahe, bas.* (Let our friendship continue. That's all.) I'll be happy. You came here. I am happy and thankful to you. I can't do this interview. It's OK, your things are. *Apne ideas hain, aap bolte rahiye, aap karte rahiye.* (Your ideas, go on talking about them, go on doing it). Three–four questions I've already enjoyed. *Nahin* (no), please.

Thapar: But Modi *sahab*.

Modi: *Nahin* please, Karan.

Thapar: But Modi *sahab*.

Modi: Karan, *dekho main dostana sambhand rakhna chahta hoon, aap usko koshish kariye.* (Look, Karan, I want to maintain good relations. You try too.)

Thapar: *Mujhe ek cheez samjhaye,* Sir. (You make me understand one thing, sir.) I am not talking about doing anything wrong. I am saying, why can't you correct your image?

Modi: This is not the time. *Uske liye aap mujhe 2002 mein mile hote, 2003 mein mile hote. Mein sab kar leta.* (For that you should have met me in 2002 or 2003. I would have done everything.)

Modi is a fast learner. He has henceforth avoided such embarrassments as the puppy analogy or running away from awkward questions on live television. And he was in his element as Gujarat's chief minister, demonstrating his political skills in running the government and in advancing the state's economic interests and development.

Nothing illustrates his chutzpah as much as his success in bringing the Tata Nano car manufacturing plant to Gujarat after it was mired in political and land acquisition-related controversies in West Bengal. He beat several other competing states by offering generous terms and the assurance of a stable labour environment. Besides, his policies for industrial growth by ensuring constant electricity supplies, installing a spectacular solar farm, innovations in quick decision-making and a business-friendly environment, led to notable economic progress.

National events were meanwhile rolling along. The Congress party under the leadership of Sonia Gandhi—assassinated Prime Minister Rajiv Gandhi's widow—wrested the central government from the National Democratic Alliance coalition led by the BJP's venerable Atal Behari Vajpayee in 2004. An effort by the BJP five years later, this time led by his chief lieutenant Lal Krishna Advani, failed to displace the Congress. Instead, the Congress increased its seats in the Lok Sabha, the lower house of Parliament.

There were moments of peril for Modi's political future. He faced murmurs of protest from Vajpayee, among others, on the 2002 murders in Gujarat. He did his own quiet lobbying and luck was with him. He survived, largely thanks to the support he could muster from some of the party's stalwarts.

THE IDEA OF INDIA

What is the idea of India?

In the first instance, it was moulded by the country's struggle for independence from British colonial rule. And the stalwarts of the independence movement mostly belonged to the Indian National Congress, although ironically it was founded by an Englishman. It was Mohandas Karamchand Gandhi—a barrister who migrated from London to South Africa to fight the apartheid regime in that country through non-violent means—who, on his return to India in 1915, gave new inspiration to the independence movement because, apart from preaching the virtues of non-violence as a means to achieve the objective of independence, he set the agenda for the Congress. He proved to be an exceptional communicator, breaking down the steps to freedom into digestible bits of symbolic and other agitations which the layman could understand.

It would be fair to say that he flummoxed the British colonial rulers by presenting the dilemmas as he did. Winston Churchill called him the 'half-naked fakir' but his authority over the independence movement was unchallenged. Whether it was Jawaharlal Nehru, Maulana Abul Kalam Azad, Sardar Vallabhbhai Patel, Chakravarti Rajagopalachari or Bhimrao Ramji 'Babasaheb' Ambedkar, the stalwarts of the independence movement sat at his feet and listened even when they disagreed with him. Only Ambedkar, the leader of the Dalits, the so-called Untouchables, dared to take issue with him publicly.

The essence of Gandhi's teachings was to ameliorate the lot of the lowest in the country's hierarchical caste system, employing non-violent means to achieve rightful ends and to try to live exemplary lives. Judging by India's religious and ethnic variety, the inbuilt legacy of the Hindu–Muslim conflict and the Muslim sway over much of contemporary India for centuries, Gandhi was careful to emphasize he imperative of communal harmony.

British India was split along the Hindu–Muslim divide in 1947, with the gathering strength of Mohammed Ali Jinnah, a brilliant lawyer, and his Muslim League. Gandhi opposed the subcontinent's partition, but the die was cast because Nehru and most other Congress leaders, ageing as they were, came to the conclusion that it was either independence with a divided subcontinent or an uncertain and dangerous future. Jinnah himself had not quite conceived of two nations in his calmer moments but he could not stop the tide of events and died not long after he became governor-general of the new nation of Pakistan.

In any case, Gandhi had decided years earlier that Nehru was to be independent India's primary leader, given his dedication to the country, his charisma and the sufferings he had undergone, together with other leaders. Patel, who was to design the unification of many princely states, technically their own masters on independence, was the other option. Gandhi rightly chose Nehru for the future benefit of the country, despite Patel being more hard-headed and a better administrator.

In the early days of partitioned India, Nehru moulded the country in line with his catholic outlook and thinking. It was a philosophy contrary to Jinnah's choice of founding a state exclusively for Muslims (although Jinnah vainly attempted to give his new nation a more secular orientation during his last days). Nehru emphasized the secular character of India and particularly sought to make Muslims welcome, despite the bloodbath on both sides in the impending partition.

It is well to remember that many leaders of the Congress, apart from Nehru, were either schooled in the West or deeply influenced by Western thought. They had imbibed the virtues of a liberal democracy, although Nehru's thinking was also shaped by the spirit of the Russian Communist revolution in its early days. Sardar Patel, on the other hand, was more homespun and had less time for theories like Communism or the other 'isms' that had intruded into the European continent.

Even before independence, there were other forces at play that were not part of the political mainstream. The RSS was founded in 1925 and sought to promote an alternative view of history and India's place in it. Its leaders presented the belief that Hindus had been corrupted by Western education and had neglected their former greatness. They opposed Gandhi because he propagated a composite culture, together with Nehru, in which Muslims were an essential part of the mix. Significantly, Nathuram Vinayak Godse, the Mahatma's assassin, was once a member of the RSS and the organization was banned for a time by none other than Sardar Patel in his capacity as home minister.

The RSS leaders opposed Nehru's constant stress on an inclusive political culture because India, in their view, was an essentially Hindu country and all permanent residents were classed as Hindus. The Sangh Parivar—the larger family of Hindu nationalist organizations affiliated to the RSS—had ideologically opposed the Partition. To buttress their case, RSS ideologues sought to dig into history to try to resuscitate the glory days of the Hindu kingdoms of yore.

Against this backdrop, where does Modi fit in? The answer can be divided into two parts: his self-esteem and the quintessentially Gujarati flair for marketing and enhancing profitability. Examples of his self-esteem are legion, most embarrassingly revealed in the pinstripe suit he wore during the visit of the president of the United States of America, Barack Obama, to India in January 2014, which had his name repeatedly woven into the stripes. When the secret was out, being the astute politician he is, he thought it best to auction the offensive suit, predictably fetching a mouth-watering amount which was passed off as being for a good cause.

Sartorially, Modi has proved to be overtly conscious. On his official trips abroad and during foreign dignitaries' visits at home, Modi undertakes several dress changes every day to suit the occasion. His trademark half-sleeved shirt is tailor-made, as are his more western-style jackets and trousers. And unlike his predecessor, who continued to display his Cross ballpoint in his breast pocket, Modi learned quickly that the modern world used the breast pocket for a vanity handkerchief, hiding pens in an insider pocket although the Indian waistcoat presented problems. Also indicative of his looks, Modi now appears perfectly coiffured, with his balding tresses of hair preened in layers at the back and his full beard trimmed to perfection.

As Gujarat's chief minister, it was Modi's self-regard that was responsible for seeking new methods of spreading campaign messages during elections. The masks with faces of leaders on them, it must be recorded, originated in the Gujarat elections and was subsequently copied by others. While Modi caught on to the possibilities of social media in enhancing his image and broadcasting his message, Twitter and Facebook were ideal for his objectives, as it promoted an instant one-way communication with his followers without the intervention of journalists asking inconvenient questions.

The 2014 general election saw a blitzkrieg that was never seen before. At great cost (party funds are not counted, although individual candidates' expenses are), the BJP employed top public relations firms, used expensive hologram technology to address manifold audiences at the same time and saturated the internet with Modi—the man and his message. The results speak for the effectiveness of the multi-million dollar campaign.

THE ALTERNATE VIEW

India's ancient civilisation has been worked on by reformers and savants of various stripes in recent centuries to create a patina of many hues, but it was Gandhi who gave the country its distinctive stamp in modern times. The essence of his teaching was Hindu in orientation. He made cleanliness next to godliness and encompassed all religions in defining the modern Indian.

Gandhi was, above all, a great communicator, and he liaised with the masses in a language and idiom they understood. The message was simple and he weaved in folk tales and myths. They could retain their favourite gods and goddesses or pray to Prophet Mohammed or Jesus Christ and still retain the 'Indianness' that was their unique characteristic.

The Hindu–Muslim divide is part of the tragic history of the subcontinent. While communal passions were aroused by vested interests or zealots in either community, Gandhi could not avert the mass murders and mayhem that followed the subcontinent's division into India and Pakistan in August 1947. It is testimony to his extraordinary life—which extended from reading for the Bar in England to practising law in South Africa while honing his skills as a votary of non-violence—that his avatar in India as the Mahatma was cut short by a Hindu fanatic. This, as we shall see, is the other strain in Indian thinking and political philosophy that has waxed and waned in the decades of independent India.

If Gandhi was the beacon of independent India in providing the modern Indian state with its moral compass and the new native rulers with the ability to communicate with the masses who took the experiment in democracy on faith, Jawaharlal Nehru, his often awkward disciple, was the architect of a practising democracy. In one sense, the mentor and his pupil were very dissimilar personalities. The former was an ascetic, apt to think in religious terms; the latter was secular, less given to explaining the country's problems in the religious idiom and passionately committed to making India both democratic and modern.

Like all great leaders, Nehru was both a romantic and a visionary. India for him was a civilisation and a new avatar of an ancient nation. He knew the shortcomings of the vehicle of the ruling party, the Indian National Congress, and the then largely illiterate masses who believed him and Gandhi regarding the efficacy of democracy in taking them and the country forward. Indeed, there was something extraordinarily touching in the illiterate villager's faith while casting his vote in the world's biggest democratic elections.

The Congress was, in many respects, an imperfect instrument of change, constituting as it did a compendium of diverse tendencies. After the tall independence leaders, came mediocrities and careerists, as was perhaps inevitable. And with time a number of leaders sought to distinguish themselves from Nehru's left-of-centre leanings and his belief in state enterprises to speed up progress and development. The stalwarts Chakravarti Rajagopalachari and Minoo Masani, to name two, were on the right of Nehruvian philosophy. But in the first decades of independence, Nehru and his philosophy held sway.

The main dissenter in the national discourse—so startlingly and tragically represented by the assassination of the Mahatma—came to be embodied by two phenomena. First was the birth of the RSS and second the persona and philosophy of Syama Prasad Mookerjee who carved out a more Hindu-centric view for the country and its politics. He founded the Bharatiya Jana Sangh (henceforth Jana Sangh) in 1951 after consulting the RSS. The proponents of these two phenomena were natural allies. Gandhi's assassin Nathuram Godse was a former member of the larger Sangh Parivar, the Akhil Bharatiya Hindu Mahasabha.

The RSS represents a stream of spartan Hindu traditions. It is, in philosophical terms, a strange mélange of wishes and naïve beliefs. Its ostentatious imitation military drills flow from the belief that Hindus were defeated by northern conquerors and then the British over the centuries because of inherent Hindu physical and mental weaknesses. Its motto, the supremacy of Hindu thought, is part of its followers' collective consciousness. The incongruity of corpulent middle-aged men in baggy shorts doing military parades each morning with staves for dummy rifles does not strike the rank and file as incongruous.

The Jana Sangh, with its initial pitiable representation of three in Parliament in 1952, came to view the RSS as its mentor and guide. Leaders of the RSS tended to think of the future in the longer term, rather than in electoral cycles. And they inducted their own trusted men reared in the RSS laboratory into the political party to give it the right leavening and exercise a measure of control. Depending upon the Jana Sangh (later christening itself the Bharatiya Janata Party in 1980) leadership and the mettle of the RSS top leader, one or the other has the whip hand. But no BJP leader dare question the ideological supremacy of the RSS, whatever his feelings.

There were, of course, other political tendencies in the early decades. The undivided Communist Party of India, the CPI, with its loyalty to Moscow as the intellectual fatherland and fount of money, was often viewed as the Congress 'B' team. In any event, the Nehruvian Congress had stolen most of its clothes. Perhaps the CPI was perceived by Muslim intellectuals as more secular than the Congress in the Hindu–Muslim divide. But the Congress could be ruthless on occasion, as was demonstrated in 1959 under Prime Minister Nehru by its sacking of the first CPI government in the state of Kerala where it had won elections in 1957.

For the Indian Communists, the country's humiliating defeat at the hands of China in the 1962 border war led to a split in the Communist movement, with a Marxist faction styling itself after the Communist Party of India (Marxist) with more pronounced Chinese sympathies. And it is due to the remarkable prowess of the new Communist party that it had a long 34-year spell of rule in West Bengal, regardless of the means adopted to stay in power.

In course of time, the ideological pulls, weak at the best of times, increasingly gave way to caste and identity politics. Initially, reservations for the Scheduled Castes in particular were based on the justifiable principle that they had been so suppressed in society on account of their status that they deserved a leg-up for an initial period in new India. But the initial ten-year reservation came to acquire a permanent character and more and more sub-sections of society came to enjoy their own reservations to the extent that identities occupied some half of the political space in competitive politics. The South was a pioneer in this respect, with the result that Brahmins, who as the high born came to face reverse discrimination, dominated the countrywide civil services because they had to move out to the northern space to secure a place in the sun.

Increasingly, caste and identity politics have come to dominate the electoral arithmetic and one of the greatest successes for a time has been Mayawati, the leader of the Dalits near the bottom of the Hindu caste scale, winning the important northern state of Uttar Pradesh for her Bahujan Samaj Party. In fact, it is now a given in most parts of the country that political strategies are built around caste arithmetic.

Inevitably, the name of Vishwanath Pratap Singh, a one-time princeling, a Congress luminary, a frequent cabinet minister and briefly prime minister, is associated with reinforcing reservations based on caste and creed in Indian politics. A commission was formed under the chairmanship of Bindeshwari Prasad Mandal in January 1979 to identify socially and educationally backward classes and consider quotas and reservations to redress caste discrimination using social indicators to determine backwardness. The Second Backward Classes Commission, it recommended 27 per cent reservation of jobs for the welfare of other backward classes, the OBCs, a collective term used by the Government of India to classify castes which are socially and educationally disadvantaged. The First Backward Classes Commission instituted in 1953 under the chairmanship of Kaka Kalelkar identified 2,399 backward castes or communities in the entire country, 837 of which were classified as the 'most backward'.

Historically disadvantaged people belonging to the Scheduled Castes and Scheduled Tribes (16.6 per cent and 8.6 per cent of the total population according to the 2011 census) were recognized by the Indian Constitution even as the caste system was abolished and Untouchability made a crime under law in 1977. Many minority religious institutions—Muslim, Sikh, Christian and Jain—have had 30–50 per cent reservations for their communities.

The manner in which reservations have run riot in the Indian system can be gauged by their relentless march. Reservations in higher education, public sector and most government bodies were raised to 49.5 per cent in 2008 by including OBCs. Women were given 50 per cent reservations in gram sabhas (village assemblies) although a bill granting 33 per cent reservation for women in the Lok Sabha and in state legislatures has languished for years in Parliament. Most political parties do not want to share a smaller pie for men.

Jawaharlal Nehru was aware of the pernicious effects of reservations. But he seemed helpless and unable to stop the bandwagon. At one point he interjected, 'Even promotions are based on communal and caste considerations. This way lies not only folly but disaster'. A cap had to be placed at 50 per cent in reservations for various categories in 1963, with at least two states, Tamil Nadu and Rajasthan, overshooting the mark at 69 per cent and 68 per cent respectively.

The passions roused by caste and its attendant effects on employment were dramatically illustrated in September 1990. While most political parties paid homage to the Mandal Commission, they wisely refrained from implementing its recommendations. It took the sincerity and punk of Vishwanath Pratap Singh to implement them. And, all hell broke loose.

Agitation against the Mandal Commission began in August 1990. The next month large sections of the middle class, professionals, lawyers and media personnel opposed the reservations. And on 19 September a student set himself on fire in Delhi, with others emulating him in several towns in Punjab, with the Army having to be called out to restore order. Strikingly, reservations were a given in south India because the Dravidian movement had set in train a reverse discrimination against Brahmins and the upper castes much earlier.

With the implementation of the Mandal Commission's recommendations, the political picture changed dramatically. The Dalits and so-called backwards of various stripes were to acquire new clout. It led to the ultimate triumph of Mayawati in Uttar Pradesh and many regional parties led by leaders such as Nitish Kumar and Lalu Prasad Yadav in Bihar and other factions with an announced or implicit caste base acquired new power. The Samajwadi Party of Uttar Pradesh was built on the bulwark of caste.

The political power of the caste movement was again brought home in more recent times in Modi's home state Gujarat with the launching of the Patel (*patidar* or land owner) movement. Ironically, Patels are a dominant community in the state and are well represented in the political power structure. But there are many among the younger generation who feel left out.

THE HINDU UNDERPINNING

It was Vinayak Damodar 'Veer' Savarkar, poet, playwright and politician, who had created the term Hindutva (literally, Hinduness) although his explanation of the concept seemed confused and contradictory. But his views on caste were singularly catholic. He wished to eliminate the caste system. He also wanted Hindu converts to be readmitted into the Hindu fold. While in jail for his anti-colonial activities, he openly espoused Hindu nationalism.

Savarkar was arrested in connection with Gandhi's assassination, in view of assassin Nathuram Godse's links with the Hindu Mahasabha, but was acquitted because the charges could not be sustained. The honour of being the co-founder of Hindutva must go to Syama Prasad Mookerjee.

Mookerjee's was a meandering journey through the Congress party and the Bengal Legislative Council in 1929 to the ranks of Jawaharlal Nehru's cabinet as a minister in the interim central government of 1947. But his inclinations were never in doubt. At one stage, he had said that if Muslims in India wanted to leave, they should pack their bags and go. Gandhi's murder cast a shadow over the Hindu Mahasabha whose president he became, though he condemned the assassination.

In 1950, after the Nehru–Liaquat Ali Khan pact to establish minority commissions, with India and Pakistan guaranteeing minority rights, Mookerjee resigned. After founding the Jana Sangh, his party contested the 1952 parliamentary election and won three seats, including his own. Mookerjee believed that the special status accorded to Jammu and Kashmir under Article 370 of the Constitution would lead to the country's Balkanisation. He later softened his stand to suggest autonomy for each of the three regions of Kashmir. He travelled to Kashmir without a permit, then a requirement, and was detained. He died in detention under mysterious circumstances on 23 June 1953. The autonomy plan was repudiated by the Jana Sangh after his death, apparently on the advice of the RSS.

The promotion of unabashed Hindu nationalism was the common theme of the co-founders. Nehru's idea of India was, in some respects, alien to the philosophy of these leaders. On the central issue of the Hindu–Muslim divide that had led to the bloody partition of the subcontinent, Hindu nationalists held views that contradicted the narrative of Gandhi, Nehru and other Congress leaders. The crux of their argument was along the following lines. It was the Muslim leaders led by Mohammed Ali Jinnah who insisted on having a separate homeland of their own. Having obtained Pakistan, Muslims who chose to remain in post-partition India could live under Hindu terms, that is, those of the majority.

On the other hand, the Congress party credo is that Muslim leaders, rather than their co-religionists or Hindus and other religious minorities, sought to divide the subcontinent. The post-1947 India remains a multi-ethnic and multi-religious nation and should give equal treatment to all Indian citizens. Periodic Hindu–Muslim riots, however, are a reminder that the wounds of Partition have not healed and bringing about Hindu–Muslim amity is very much a work in progress.

Hindu nationalists point to terror attacks on India instigated by Pakistan not only in Kashmir but also in the rest of the country. The most spectacular and deadly of recent attacks was in Mumbai in 2008 in which 166 people were killed. There is sufficient evidence to nail its origin to Pakistan. The cheerleaders and masterminds of the plot remain free in Pakistan and continue to spout anti-Indian vitriol. Part of Pakistan's problem is that some of the terrorists that state agencies nurtured to keep India off balance have come to bite the hand that fed them. Besides, Pakistan's spy agencies now tend to divide terrorists into the good and bad varieties; the former target India, while the latter attack Pakistani targets and assets. The main spy agency traditionally enjoys great autonomy. On the rebound, there is growing attraction for the BJP's tooth-for-tooth approach towards Pakistan.

The muscularity of the Hindu nationalist view of Pakistan and, up to a point, China is viewed by the BJP as an asset in swinging votes. Continuing criticism of the Congress-led governments' allegedly soft, if not supine, conduct of foreign policy was an important element of attack by Narendra Modi and other BJP leaders in the campaign rhetoric of the 2014 general elections. For the layman, there is an obvious appeal for a tough policy with adversarial nations, if not the wider world.

PRIVATE PERSON

Despite his passion for propagating brand Modi, he likes to keep his private life, private. He is fond of broadcasting the myth of having been a *chaiwala* as a young boy, helping his father run a railway tea stall, for its political effect. In fact, a faux pas by a Congress leader during the general election campaign of 2014 alluding to his tea-boy antecedents was used to telling effect by the BJP in inaugurating a new public forum christened *chai pe charcha* (conversations over tea).

But Narendra Modi has never explained how he chose to abandon his young wife Jashodaben Chimanlal—the two were apparently engaged as toddlers—whom he hardly knew in search of his own salvation by wandering around the country for years. According to published reports, Modi left his wife after three years of marriage, of which they lived together for only three months. And in all the years he was in the RSS and the BJP at various levels of responsibility, he has not acknowledged his wife, except in filing his last election papers in April 2014 in which he said he was married. Even during his long spell as Gujarat's chief minister, in his largely sedentary life, he chose not to live with his wife.

After he became prime minister, his wife publicly expressed her desire to join him and serve as his official hostess in Delhi. Modi's response was silence. After assuming office he went to seek his mother's blessings as a dutiful son. Missing from the scene was his lonely wife. She is a retired school teacher and reportedly receives a pension of Rs 14,000 a month.

Yet, Jashodaben was provided a security detail in Gujarat as the prime minister's wife, at which she expressed her annoyance and hope that her husband would ask her to live with him one day.

Is Modi's conduct determined by his desire not to be encumbered by a wife he hardly knows? Or is he trying to make the political point that he is so dedicated to his responsibilities that he does not wish family responsibilities to come in the way? We will not know until he chooses to break his silence. A cynical criticism of his behaviour would be that nothing and no one should come in the way of his persona to shine as the country's prime minister.

In confirmation, Modi's appeal for votes to the Gujarat assembly election in February 2002—writes Kingshuk Nag in his book *The NaMo Story: A Political Life*—was couched in the following terms: 'I am an honest man, vote for me. I cannot be dishonest. I don't have a family'.

Modi's first term in office has given us an inkling of his method of governance. He is quick at taking decisions. He has built a strong Prime Minister's Office to oversee the government's functioning. He gives his officers much leeway as long as they perform well according to his norms. His inner circle consists of barely three persons, his acolyte and fellow Gujarati Amit Shah elevated to the BJP presidency, Arun Jaitley, the finance minister, and Rajnath Singh, the home minister.

Officials in his entourage are known for their personal loyalty to him. This is a trait he shares with Indira Gandhi, the heroine of the 1971 Bangladesh War. In fact, many members of the middle and professional classes admire him, as they had admired her, for providing strong leadership.

Like any successful politician, Modi can be ruthless in the pursuit of his goals and throws conventions to the winds. For instance, he campaigned in key state assembly elections after assuming the prime minister's mantle. His electoral rhetoric was unusually sharp against his political opponents without regard for his high national office. In effect, he diminished his national stature for partisan ends. He was, of course, seeking to augment the BJP's seat share in the Rajya Sabha, the upper house of Parliament, based on his party's strength in state legislatures, where it is in a minority.

FASTS AND AGITATIONS

Fasts and agitations were integral to the vocabulary of the Indian independence movement. They were sanctified by Mahatma Gandhi who encouraged non-violent agitations for a cause. He would often go on fast either to highlight a demand he considered just or simply as a form of self-penance if he had transgressed. Often, non-violent agitations did not hold and he would call them off whenever they turned violent.

Jaya Prakash Narayan was moulded in the tradition of Gandhi's philosophy. A man once considered Jawaharlal Nehru's heir, he was singularly inimical to power and believed in productive social and political reform. He promoted the cause of an alternative Indian polity because of his belief that the Westminster model adopted for governing independent India was not entirely suited to her genius and idiom. His probity and integrity were bywords and JP, as he was universally known, had earned the popular title of 'Lok Nayak' (people's hero).

With Vithal Mahadeo Tarkunde, another social reformer, JP founded Citizens for Democracy in 1974 and the People's Union for Civil Liberties in 1976—non-governmental organizations to uphold and defend civil rights. Inevitably, as Indira Gandhi lurched towards an authoritarian bent of mind, JP led the Nav Nirman Andolan (Reconstruction Movement) of Gujarat, a precursor to what was to come in Delhi. At a massive rally, he declared that the 'country was wracked by hunger, rising prices, corruption...oppressed by every kind of injustice. It is a Total Revolution we want, nothing less'.

Somewhat rashly, JP asked the military and the police to disregard the government's 'unconstitutional and immoral orders', an imprecise and combustible peroration. After Indira Gandhi was found guilty of a technical violation of an electoral law by a court, he asked her to resign. Instead, she imposed a state of internal Emergency. He, together with many other leaders, was placed under detention.

It was in this spirit of conducting agitations through fasts and great gatherings that Anna Hazare burst on the national scene in 2011. He had the rather unlikely background of being a former Indian army corporal whose function was to drive trucks. He had retired from the army years ago and devoted his spartan life in his home village of Ralegan Siddhi in Mahrashtra to the welfare of the people, disciplining drunkards by tying them to trees as well as engaging in more purposeful activities by calling politicians at the provincial level to account and improving the lives of his village folk.

In moving to the national stage, he fastened on the theme of an all-powerful Lokpal (ombudsman) as an anti-corruption measure and to hold the government to account. His demands were extravagant and, if followed literally, would have negated the Indian Constitution. In the national capital and the rest of the country, he had built up sufficient steam to emerge as a major national figure out to slay the dragon of hydra-headed corruption.

Anna's supporters grew exponentially and vast crowds thronged his jamborees, the climax of which was the Gandhian staple, declaring a fast until death unless his demands were met. The setting was the Ramlila grounds in Delhi and as he fasted in full public view propped up by round pillows, the political crisis mounted. Government ministers came to parley and ultimately the government agreed to organize a round table of discussions between a clutch of senior cabinet ministers and representatives of Anna.

A Lokpal Bill—a far paler version of what he had wanted—was introduced in Parliament as Anna took time off, warning that he would go on fast again if the bill continued to languish without being passed into law. He would undertake another fast, this time back in Ralegan Siddhi, to ensure passage of the bill. And he was true to his word by going on an indefinite fast in December 2013. More importantly, the fast did the trick and the bill was passed with the help of the principal opposition party, the BJP and other groups, except for the Samajwadi Party, a caste-based socialist faction of Uttar Pradesh.

One of the key supporters of Anna was Arvind Kejriwal, a one-time tax official who had branched out as a social reformer and would become an enthusiastic supporter of Anna's anti-corruption crusade. Anna was in the genre of timeless Indian reformers who shunned the political world to achieve their goals through mass movements. Indeed, the world of politics was anathema to Anna. Kejriwal, on the other hand, held the view that one had to enter the political system to reform it from within.

INDIRA'S TRIUMPH AND TRAGEDY

.

Nehru's long and eventful innings at the helm of the nation came to an end in 1964. He was, in fact, the primary architect of independent India. His greatest contribution was to give his country a democratic underpinning. He introduced the building of major dams and steel mills and both by inclination and necessity he favoured state intervention for the modernisation of India.

In foreign policy, he carved out a special place for India in retaining autonomy, given the very modest military power she possessed. The Non-Aligned Movement (NAM) was the answer although in practice New Delhi had little option but to tilt towards Moscow in view of Pakistan's status as a United States ally and China's flexing of muscles along the disputed mountainous border. The NAM served an ideological need until it was overwhelmed by the avalanche of the Sino-Indian border war of 1962, with a desperate India seeking military assistance from the United States. Given Washington's niggardly response, Nehru tried to recover his balance somewhat after the Chinese had declared a unilateral ceasefire.

But the greatest challenge to democratic India was posed by Nehru's daughter Indira Gandhi. Nehru was followed by an all too brief reign of the Congress party apparatchik Lal Bahadur Shastri, who was in turn followed by Indira. In what has now become political folklore, she was installed by the Congress party in the belief that she could be manipulated; that she was, in effect, a *goongi gudiya* (dumb doll), a description attributed to socialist leader Ram Manohar Lohia Indeed, her initial moves as prime minister were tentative and hesitant and much was made of her influential advisers, popularly dubbed the kitchen cabinet.

Little did the Congress party bosses know what was in store for them. She engineered two splits in the party to be her own boss, bringing into the Indian political scene Communist methods of propaganda. She unleashed a virtual avalanche of populist rhetoric tilted towards a seemingly left ideology capped by the nationalisation of banks. Slogans became the order of the day, but their underlying purpose was to demolish the hold of the traditional party bosses. Her Congress became the Congress-I, where 'I' stood for Indira while the rump Congress converted itself into the Congress-O, where 'O' stood for organization.

Indira went on to win the 1971 war with Pakistan over the creation of Bangladesh. The then military rulers of Pakistan thought their best bet was the suppression of the autonomy movement in the province of East Pakistan which morphed into the independence movement. By all accounts, the Pakistan army and its representatives were brutal in dealing with Bengali protesters and committed unspeakable atrocities.

Millions of Bangladeshi refugees poured into India giving New Delhi a loud stake in the outcome. East Pakistani leaders were given shelter in India with the men receiving military training in the neighbouring state of West Bengal. Indira played her diplomatic cards with great finesse, travelling to the United States and West Europe to warn world leaders of an impending conflagration, given India's inability to care for millions of refugees. And as a safety valve, India came closest to repudiating its non-aligned creed by signing an Indo–Soviet military treaty.

Pakistan was foolish enough to provoke a military conflict, with the almost inevitable defeat and surrender of its army in East Pakistan. The then Soviet Union guarded India's flank in the United Nations Security Council while the short battle between the two countries lasted. And Bangladesh as an independent nation was born.

Often in history, a great triumph is followed by an unexpected reverse, and Indira's difficulties seemed to multiply with each passing day. Opposition to Indira and the Congress coalesced around the figure of Jaya Prakash Narayan or JP, a reluctant revolutionary who gave voice to the sense of deep gloom in the country, at one time rashly suggesting that the police and other organs of the state should refuse to follow the government's 'illegal' orders. Parleys were held between JP and the government but there seemed no meeting ground. Indira's followers opted for their own counter-protests in answer to growing anti-government mass meetings.

And then it happened. On the morning of 26 June 1975 a countrywide state of national Emergency was declared. All the major opposition leaders had been arrested, a press censorship was imposed and a vicious birth control drive under the auspices of Indira's younger son Sanjay was unleashed in Delhi. In one fell swoop, Indira was seemingly destroying her father's life work in constructing a democratic country. It is a different matter that the trains ran on time and in the initial phase the lackadaisical work-force of junior civil servants was punctual in attending office.

It was a strange atmosphere in the country. But for a few exceptions, a free and often rumbustious press ate out of the government's hand, most political activity fell silent and a nation nurtured on Nehru's copious diet of democracy became supine. It was not a situation that could last indefinitely, but while it lasted it made one wonder how deep and enduring the architecture of democratic India was.

And then, as suddenly as the Emergency had been announced,

Indira sprang a surprise by ordering fresh elections, with the opposition leaders released and the press breathing free again, with newspapers that had been most subservient breathing fire and brimstone. The rest, as they say, is history. Indira and her Congress were humiliatingly defeated and the disparate opposition leaders and parties that had come to fight her were suddenly thrown together. Thus began a new saga in India's political development.

16 DECEMBER 2012

One date marks a dramatic turn in the collective Indian consciousness. On 16 December 2012 a young physiotherapy student and her male friend took a bus at night after watching a movie in a central New Delhi district. It was a private bus, one of the many that ply the capital's streets without a licence after duty hours and try to earn a little extra for the driver and his staff by taking in passengers.

India is a predominantly conservative society. The erotic friezes of Khajuraho and the famous Kama Sutra guide to sex might have titillated and fascinated the rest of the world, but the bulk of today's India is steeped in conservatism. Waves of reformers over at least two centuries have added different patinas of morality and modesty, and they have cumulatively given the average Indian a Victorian sensibility.

The home of a typical Indian politician reflects his or her make-up. With pictures and figurines of gods and goddesses of the gaudiest variety are a refrigerator in the sitting room, the inevitable television set decorated with an embroidered cover for the top, photographs of the host with political notables and chairs with assorted embroidered cushions. And in every home, table lamps are capped by shades that are three sizes too small, singularly lacking in any sense of aesthetics.

One is left wondering where the great aesthetic sense of our ancestors has disappeared.

A BJP politician is the best representative of the newly urbanized middle-class owing to his nativist beliefs. He rails at foreign (read Western) influences. He is consciously native, worships an army of mythical images and wears his nationalism on his sleeve. He is, by his own account, a nationalist, the son of the soil and takes pride in being true to his traditional culture and values.

In gender terms, the average Indian politician believes in male supremacy, whatever the Indian Constitution might say. He is the breadwinner and the family's provider and the women of the family in the shape of wife and daughters must obey his command. The wife must cook and look after the house; the daughters must study up to a point and dutifully marry the men of their fathers' choice. Any violation of the code invites retribution. In the rural areas of Haryana and Punjab in particular, such retribution takes the form of 'honour killings', usually of the erring daughter and often also of the man she wanted to marry. In any event, girls are viewed as a burden because their marriage involves a dowry that penalizes parents while subjecting the bride to harassment at the hands of the in-laws in case the dowry is deemed insufficient. The ultimate punishment, sometimes, for the bride is that she is burned to death.

There is a different India taking shape at the same time: the modern and rebellious men and women who view many of the traditional values as old wives' tales and seek to go their own way. In the end, the bulk of the rebellious compromise by marrying the person they love in the traditional fat Indian wedding, its scale depending upon the prosperity of the girl's parents or their ability to raise back-breaking loans.

There are inevitable clashes between the young and old as there are in every society, but in India's traditional world overlaid with shades of Victorian morality, such clashes tend to be ugly and often fatal. In essence then, Indian society is patriarchal, deeply conservative and whatever the laws might say, heaves to its own patriarchal values. Rapes are all too frequent occurrences, compounded as they are of a dangerous cocktail of semi-educated men let loose in towns and cities and fed on the mushy romances of the typical Bollywood film. They are too poor and too rustic to find sex except through force. But a larger percentage of rape cases are committed by relations or friends of the victim, vicariously satisfying their sexual urges the easy way, in an ostensibly moralistic and hypocritical society.

That December night, the driver and his helpers made a macabre feast of it by incapacitating the male companion and raping the girl most brutally and repeatedly while navigating New Delhi's streets before throwing her and her companion out of the moving bus, and on the road. A police van finally picked up the hapless couple and unlike the vast majority of cases, all hell broke loose. It was in part the pathos of it, a young small town girl wishing to make good in the big city by becoming a professional, enjoying the innocent pleasure of watching a film with a companion. Also, it was the accumulation of frustration for the young who simply had had enough.

And the young rebelled as never before. On the expansive lawns of India Gate, there was a sea of humanity of the young and a smattering of elderly supporters wishing to make the point that they could not go on living as they had. The police used water cannons and batons to try to bring some order to the rebellious swelling crowds. But the young were undeterred. They took the blows and the cannons in their stride and would not be deterred. They held candlelight vigils night after night, and these drills were repeated in many cities and towns across the country.

One salutary result of this mass anger—the unfortunate victim died from her grievous wounds in a Singapore hospital—was the appointment of a commission under a retired Chief Justice of the

Supreme Court, which presented a sterling report stiffening the law against harassment of women, promptly adopted by Parliament. But in a striking illustration of the limited utility of laws, a photo-journalist and her male companion were waylaid on the grounds of a derelict textile mill in Mumbai not that long afterwards, to be set upon by men after rendering the companion harmless.

The problem, of course, is that male attitudes formed over decades and centuries cannot change overnight. Besides, there is a dichotomy of views in Hindu mythology. Besides submissive and dutiful wives, there is a special place in Hindu mythical tales for strong women, some of them taking the form of the destroyer, others as warriors for territory or honour. In fact, in the popular mind, the woman as mother is revered and worshipped and in such a role she can do no wrong.

On the hoods of scooter rickshaws that ply the Delhi roads are often painted the simple word Ma (Mother) or, more elaborately, the prescription, Ma Ka Aashirwad (Mother's Benediction). And in the freedom struggle, a rallying cry was Bharat Mata Ki Jai (Victory to Mother India), an adage that continues to figure in political demonstrations of various kinds. It is as if having sublimated the mother as a goddess, men feel free to abuse her in various ways. The suppression of women is not unique to Indian society. It exists in many other societies and nations, but it is nonetheless curious that a civilisation as ancient, aesthetic and erudite as India's should have degenerated into the parody it has become as far as treatment of women is concerned. The modern politician's trite comment is that people's mindset needs to be changed.

Telescoping history, after Arvind Kejriwal's impressive landslide win in the re-election to the Delhi assembly—with the Aam Aadmi Party (AAP) capturing 67 of the 70 seats, the remaining three going to the BJP—came a shocker. In advertising AAP's achievements through an elaborate propaganda commercial spot liberally shown on private television news channels, Kejriwal, who likes to consider himself as something of a revolutionary, shows his own anti-woman bent.

The commercial spot begins with a housewife apparently belonging to the lower middle-class lamenting the high cost of living. She is shown buying vegetables, returning a cauliflower she cannot afford. She cooks food for her husband sitting in an armchair watching television. Next she brings the new electricity bill with a sharply reduced amount to her husband, still immobile in his chair, and praises Kejriwal for reducing the bill for modest customers. She brings the food tray to her husband who is still watching television, while she sits opposite not to join him for a meal but to launch into a lecture on how all must come to the aid of Kejriwal's AAP.

FOREIGN POLICY SURPRISE

The biggest surprise of Modi's first year in office has been his major moves in the foreign policy field. As Gujarat's chief minister, he had journeyed twice to China and to Japan. His fascination with these two countries was understandable. They are two Asian countries that have taken the leap into the modern industrial age. He sought to find out their secrets and also to tempt them to invest in his state. With the United States, with which he shared a natural affinity in a shared entrepreneurial spirit and business-friendly instincts, he silently bore the cross of being denied entry after the anti-Muslim pogrom in Gujarat in 2002.

However, few had suspected Modi of possessing the political acumen and understanding of the complex field of foreign relations. He started with a bang by inviting the executive heads of all of India's neighbours, members of SAARC (South Asian Association for Regional Cooperation) to his swearing-in ceremony on 26 May 2014. All Indian prime ministers have paid homage to SAARC, but none had thought of making a dramatic gesture to emphasize the point that the country's foreign policy starts with cultivating good relations with its neighbours.

To no one's surprise, the complex nature of the troubled relationship with Pakistan asserted itself soon, but Modi's starting point of inviting Pakistan's prime minister, Nawaz Sharif, and his acceptance was noted in the world's capitals. In fact, relations with Pakistan turned out to be his Achilles' heel. He had called off a dialogue in 2014 at the last minute on the specious ground that Pakistan was hosting the separatist Hurriyat movement of Kashmir at their New Delhi High Commission before the formal talks with India, a practice routinely followed by Islamabad. His flip-flop attitude was perhaps determined by playing to the national gallery, his party supporters in particular.

Apparently, it took time for Modi to retrace his steps. After blowing hot and cold, he took the opportunity of the Pakistan prime minister's presence at a regional summit in a Russian setting to unveil an ambitious set of meetings, in addition to stating that the two countries would fight terrorism jointly. How sustainable this new approach will be, time will tell, but it holds the promise of an extended dialogue underlining the premise that only a consistent dialogue not necessarily at the summit level, despite the risks, is the way to a peaceful subcontinent. The nature of Indo–Pakistan relations being what they are, the bonhomie in Russia soon turned into a familiar pattern of mutual recrimination.

As a token of Modi's wider vision, he used his Russian journey to visit the five 'stans' in Central Asia that became independent on the break-up of the Soviet Union. These new nations are the object of China's attention, particularly with an eye on its new 'silk road' initiative. In view of India's historical links with the region, closer relations between New Delhi and the 'stans', many of them resource-rich, signified by a prime ministerial visit should be mutually beneficial.

Modi's second starting point in foreign policy was that despite the humiliation heaped upon him by denying him a visa for years, a pillar of the country's relationship in the post-Cold War world was to build strong vibes with the United States. Here again Modi's out-of-the-box thinking helped. His invitation to President Barack Obama to be the chief guest at India's Republic Day on 26 January 2015 military parade hit the bull's eye.

More importantly, Modi was able to build a personal rapport with President Obama, as was clear from his own visit to the United States and their extensive conversations. These discussions were continued during the extended talks between the two leaders, most notably on the lawns of Hyderabad House (the state guest house) in New Delhi, a session that also highlighted the prime minister's custom-made pinstripe suit.

Apart from visiting neighbours, among the first foreign visits Modi made was to Japan. In ideological terms, Modi and Japan's prime minister, Shinzo Abe, are made for each other. Both are ideologically right, both are for giving business full opportunities, both seek closer defence relations. Modi's admiration for the military and technological rise of an Asian power in a West-dominated age, despite the evil use it was put to in World War II, is understandable. Equally understandable is his desire to tap Tokyo for large investments and transfer of technology.

With China, India lives with the legacy of the disastrous 1962 border war, the unresolved border dispute, Beijing's emergence as an aspiring Great Power, its close relations with Pakistan with an eye on India and the burgeoning and lopsided trade relationship. Modi grasped the point that merely nursing grievances against China will lead nowhere. The only sane policy is to negotiate and interact with Beijing while holding India's head high. Privately, India's conversations with the Chinese leadership have taken on a more robust tone. In a sense, Modi's visit accomplished these objectives against the backdrop of President Xi Jinping's own visit to India in 2014, marred by a substantial Chinese troop incursion into India across the border.

In June 2015, Modi completed a successful visit to Bangladesh, of which the high point was the ratification of the land boundary accord exchanging enclaves in each other's territory with their residents given the choice of citizenship. It was signed more than 40 years ago and immediately ratified by Dhaka. But it languished for more than four decades because New Delhi did not pass the required constitutional amendment, partly because of the resistance of the BJP, then in opposition.

Perhaps Modi overplayed his hand by taking a swipe at Pakistan in his parting address to the civic community in Dhaka by pointing to the then Pakistan government's and army's role in suppressing the Bangladesh independence movement. And he indulged in a bombastic comparison between the land border agreement and the fall of the Berlin Wall.

Another innovation Modi introduced into his Asian travels was to emphasize the civilisational links of Buddhism, India being the springboard of the creed, in addition to the spread of Hinduism in the East. Second, even as Gujarat's chief minister, Modi had highlighted the role of the Indian diaspora in promoting the mother country's development and in carrying the Indian flag in their new homes around the world.

Although he had a point in seeking to use the diaspora as an additional element in promoting New Delhi's interests, Modi stumbled in one respect. It is a wise convention that a leader visiting another country in his official capacity does not denigrate his domestic political opponents on foreign soil.

Yet time and again, in addressing Indians of the NRI (non-resident Indian) or the PIO (persons of Indian origin) varieties in New York, Australia and Beijing, Modi made a crudely partisan pitch by congratulating himself and his government and deriding the work and policies of his Congress predecessors.

Apart from Pakistan, perhaps Modi met his match in reshaping the country's policy towards Israel. He will be walking into a minefield when he visits Israel, becoming the first Indian prime minister to do so. The coalition Israeli prime minister, Benjamin Netanyahu, heads is the most extreme right-wing government to take office in the nation's history. Second, the BJP has cultivated a symbiotic relationship with Israel because of its spiritual affinity for its leaders' tooth-for-tooth approach to its adversaries and their anti-Muslim stance. The BJP's special relationship with Israel was in full display in the RSS weekly *Organiser* of June 2015. In an opinion piece by Rajnikant Purohit it carried, Israel is extolled as a 'great nation'. He wrote:

> There are some who argue that since the Jews were most harassed in Europe and the Holocaust was caused by Hitler's Germany, Israel should have been created in Europe rather than in the Middle East…Well, the Jews have been at the receiving end of the Muslims too for centuries. Besides, the area of Israel and the West Bank (Judea and Samaria) and Jerusalem is truly the Biblical area of the Jews where all their holy places exist. So locating Israel where it is currently located was fully justified.

Purohit was in a particularly generous mood and suggested that Europeans should carve out a second Israel for Jews in Europe as a form of penance for what they did to Jews. As if on cue, India for the first time abstained in the UN Human Rights Council vote which called for Israel and Palestine to prosecute both the parties for war crimes in the 2014 Gaza war. Expectedly, the United States voted against while 41 countries, including most of Europe, voted for the adoption of the report. India was in the august company of Kenya, Ethiopia, Paraguay and Macedonia in abstaining. India's official spokesman lamely argued that there had been no change in New Delhi's policy.

Israel likes to present itself as a beleaguered country and its reference point remains the Holocaust, despite the fact that it is today a colonial power ruling over millions of Palestinians it has disenfranchised, appropriating vast areas of the West Bank to build settlements, annexing East Jerusalem, and is showing no inclination to make peace on equitable terms. As a consequence, Israel has been feeling increasingly isolated in the Western world, particularly in Europe, with the 'boycott, divestment and sanctions' (BDS) movement gaining traction.

Essentially, the aim of BDS is to pull back Western investment from Israeli establishments working out of the occupied West Bank and ban goods manufactured there by Israeli entities. Even some American universities have divested from Israeli West Bank establishments, although the American Jewish lobby remains strong and continues to frustrate all attempts at seeking a just peace. A minority pro-Israel but pro-peace 'J Street' faction has broken away from the hardline majority.

Modi has to bear in mind that coupling his Israel visit with a trip to the Palestinian territories will not compensate for his befriending Israeli prime minister, Benjamin Netanyahu, because there is no equivalence between the two. India has a growing defence relationship with Israel because of the excellence and innovative qualities of its military products. But it is one thing to establish business relations with Tel Aviv for realpolitik reasons and quite another to build a special relationship with a government even many of the Western nations have come to view as an embarrassment in the post-colonial era. Modi can hold his nose and do defence deals—the stance that President Obama has adopted in generously rearming Egypt despite President Abdel Fattah el-Sisi's autocratic rule and suppression of dissent, or make a celebration of his planned path-breaking Israeli venture.

India's stakes in the Arab world are immense not only in the employment it provides to Indians but also as a source of energy supplies. Therefore, it was entirely appropriate that Modi should have paid a visit to the United Arab Emirates, the largest trade partner of India in the Arab world. True, some Arab countries are involved in 'under-the-counter' deals with Tel Aviv and there are affinities in the new and changing geopolitical picture in the Middle East with the emergence of the Islamic State. But they do not take away the bitterness of Israel ruling as an old colonial power in the twenty-first century.

There is some merit in the present stalemate between Israel and Palestine. The pretence of holding peace talks with little or no real movement had falsely lulled the world for decades. Netanyahu makes no pretence of making peace and said so during his last election campaign. However bad his relations with President Obama may be, he is immune to American penalties or to cuts in the highest military and other assistance Washington gives any nation because of the American Jewish lobby and the support Israel enjoys in both houses of the United States Congress.

I had met Netanyahu in Israel in 1990 when he was the junior foreign minister and he had made his points forcefully. In particular, he told me, 'If you run across the breadth of Israel, you would cross it in a few hours', to stress the geographic limits of his country. Until recently, the conventional wisdom was that any peace deal would entail the retention of major Israeli settlements in exchange for territories in Israel proper and that Jerusalem would be the shared capital of two states, with the future West Bank demilitarized.

Such a scenario has now receded into never-never land, with Israel determined to keep all the land it occupied in the 1967 war and the annexed East Jerusalem, with the dreadful and untenable prospect of keeping Palestinians subjugated even though such an arrangement would see a Palestinian majority in a future Israel.

The tragedy is while the United States will not permit anyone else, least of all the United Nations, to take a lead role in negotiating peace, it is handicapped domestically and has geopolitical interests to play the role of a genuine peacemaker. The 2013–14 Israeli–Palestinian peace talks at the behest of United States secretary of state, John Kerry, was the last serious attempt to revive a dead peace process and it ended up in the wilderness. If the Republicans win the American presidency in 2017, Netanyahu will have even less to worry about.

With the prospect of Netanyahu receiving support from India in the shape of the first prime ministerial visit, Tel Aviv and its American friends are already in a celebratory mood, with a section of legislators from the United States proposing a three-way defence arrangement with Israel and India.

India's intrusion into the Middle East minefield can therefore have unpredictable consequences and Modi will have to watch his steps before indulging in his penchant for showmanship. Many mediators from many nations have met their Waterloo in trying to make peace between the colonial power and its Palestinian subjects. Netanyahu has now pronounced that he does not want third parties to help make peace and has rudely dismissed the efforts of the French foreign minister, Laurent Fabius, in seeking to initiate talks.

Thus far, Indian policy towards Israel, has been to underplay the relationship while seeking defence material and help in areas of agricultural cultivation. Modi's visit will give it a new salience at a time the Western world is becoming increasingly concerned with the direction Netanyahu and his supporters even more to his right are taking the country.

Israel has launched a full-scale war on the BDS movement because it is beginning to hurt economically and is helping to build an unflattering picture of Israel in the West. Incidents of anti-Semitism in Europe are increasing. France's desire to show it is doing something for Israeli–Palestinian rapprochement flows from the fact that it hosts the highest proportion of Jewish population in Europe.

A NEW PHENOMENON

The AAP turned the logic of a string of social and civil rights movements on its head. Even the most successful of them in recent times, Anna Hazare's 'India Against Corruption', which finally yielded a version of the Lokpal Bill passed by Parliament and now a law, sought to influence the authorities from the outside. Such movements, in Arvind Kejriwal's view, had limited usefulness, and he therefore decided that he would dirty his hands to reform society and governance from the inside.

Kejriwal chose legislative elections in Delhi as his experiment with politics for good reasons. As the country's capital, it has nationwide exposure and consists of a rather heterogeneous population concentrated in one largely urban centre. Besides, AAP had limited resources and manpower and initially needed to test its message on a small scale.

Perhaps the AAP leaders themselves were surprised by their success one year after they had formed the party with the broom symbol. The BJP, which was all but ready to take over power after three continuous spells of Congress rule under the mother figure of Sheila Dikshit, secured the largest number of seats at 31 in a house of 70 in the December 2013 elections. But the ruling Congress was reduced to a pitiable seven, with Dikshit losing her seat to Kejriwal. The AAP nudged the BJP with 28 seats.

It was a spectacular debut performance with few parallels. How did the new kid on the block achieve it? It was, above all, the moral high ground AAP took by inviting donations and publicizing them, doing house to house calls on voters, making promises to reduce water and electricity bills that it sought to fulfil. It was not so much the new party's manifesto and promises that struck a chord with voters as its apparent sincerity and the many symbolisms of being the common man's party, as its name broadcast.

Like all bold ventures, it was a gamble that paid off handsomely because above all and beyond the staple diet of the Nehruvian left-of-centre chestnuts, the streak of idealism shone through. In a democratic system in which traditional values had eroded, corruption was rife and, in what mattered to the common man, petty corruption in transacting daily tasks pinched the most, here was a party whose leaders said they would not seek spacious colonial bungalows or fleets of cars with red beacons but would rather patronize the Delhi Metro. To drive home the point, Kejriwal would use his own modest Maruti Suzuki WagonR car, apparently gifted by a supporter. Above all, it was the streak of idealism in the cynical world of politics that enthused voters and gave them that rare commodity, hope. Thus a party born yesterday felled giants, and walked home with the government of Delhi.

The BJP was simply too constrained to use the traditional method of plundering other parties to make up a majority. The Congress, shell-shocked to be reduced to a footnote after governing Delhi for fifteen years, put its thinking cap on and decided to support an AAP government to avoid a re-election and keep the BJP out. But AAP said it would stake to form a government only after going back to the voters to ask their approval through local meetings, SMSs and a telephone referendum, a peculiar interpretation of representative government.

The result was an overwhelming 'yes', and strong on symbolism, Kejriwal used the Delhi Metro to commute part of the way to his swearing-in ceremony where a fleet of cars was waiting for him and the function, in fulfilling the new governing party's desire, was held on Ramlila grounds, the very setting in which Anna Hazare had held his famous anti-corruption rally.

The new Kejriwal government did provide free water to a limit and halved power rates for modest consumers within days of coming to power, measures criticized by the other parties for the haste with which they were implemented and the greater burden they would impose on the state's budget. But Kejriwal's overriding priority was to demonstrate that, unlike other leaders, he was true to his word. However, he was quickly reminded that there were limits to symbolism. Having foresworn his predecessor's capacious colonial bungalow, he was allotted a twin five-bedroom duplex to encounter murmurs of protest from some of his own followers. He was initially operating out of his modest apartment in the unfashionable Ghaziabad district of the National Capital Region. After some prevarication, he sought more ample accommodation.

Encouraged by the Delhi triumph, with countrywide general elections months away, Kejriwal and his party set their sights high. They would go national, contesting as many as a hundred seats, a figure upped to 400 in the 542-seat Lok Sabha. The target seemed far too high although they sought to minimize their handicaps by networking with similarly inclined civic organizations and movements and signing up notables in civic movements and areas of expertise. It was an indication of how the AAP phenomenon had inspired a variety of top-level functionaries and professionals that many came forward to offer their services or join the party.

But Kejriwal proved to be a man in a hurry and, drunk on the enthusiasm his fledgling party created across the nation, he gave the impression that he would conquer the country. Wisely, he had ruled himself out of contesting a seat for the Lok Sabha even as some of his avid followers had pitched him for seeking the very top job, that of prime minister. And then he hinted he might seek the highest office, instead of making a success of his new administration in the capital.

Indeed, AAP took a few tumbles in its new avatar as a government. He had announced a Janata Darbar, a public assembly, in which any citizen could come to ventilate his grievances before the chief minister and his cabinet. Half way through this exercise, the ministerial team had to be evacuated by police because the sheer crush of an impatient public led to a near riot. Kejriwal had to give up the entire exercise and seek the avenues of the internet and telephone communication to receive public grievances. Holding assemblies of this kind is not a novel idea; two chief ministers, in Kerala and Bihar states, have been organizing them for years, winning the former a United Nations award.

Kejriwal also sought to slay the monster of corruption by making every citizen a private detective, urging him to conduct sting operations through mobile telephone and recording equipment and report the case to a designated number. And in a foolish exercise reminiscent of a vigilante raid, a minister of his government undertook a night journey to an area in which it was alleged that a group of African women were indulging in a drug and sex racket.

As usual, the minister in question was travelling with media in tow, the oxygen of AAP, and the police having declined the minister's request because they did not have a warrant, the party's volunteers took the law into their own hands and imprisoning a group of women in a taxi for hours, forced them to take a test in a medical facility while AAP volunteers shouted racist epithets. In the end, the external affairs ministry was left holding the baby, apologizing to the African diplomatic corps for the conduct of the novice ministers in the Delhi government.

Among the hasty decisions taken by the Kejriwal government was to revoke the permission given by the previous Congress government to allow foreign direct investment in multi-brand retail, a contentious issue in the Indian political space because of the argument that it would destroy the livelihood of a legion of petty shopkeepers. True, it featured in AAP's manifesto, which was a somewhat incoherent document redolent of many of the original left-of-centre Nehruvian policies largely given up by the Congress in favour of market-friendly mechanisms.

Inevitably, some of the notables from business and industry who had joined AAP raised their flags of dissent. Even more damaging to the new party was another sign of dissent, the rebellion of a Delhi legislator who characterized Kejriwal as a dictator and said he would protest against the party's failure to fulfil its promises. Kejriwal responded by accusing the dissident of seeking a ministerial post in the Delhi government and later asking for a ticket to contest the Lok Sabha election. Indeed, the traditional malaise of established parties, dissidence by members denied plum posts, surfaced in AAP remarkably early.

Kejriwal is media-savvy, and, realizing that his party was appearing in less than a glorious role, given its succession of stumbles, he gave a series of interviews to major television channels retailing the record of its short rule and taking the offensive in fighting for his baby. He was less than convincing but he made it known that there was plenty of fight left in him.

The hope and promise AAP engendered towards the end of a decade of Congress government was in itself a truly remarkable phenomenon. Its underlying implication was even more promising. Given a suitable vehicle, there were many men and women and organizations in the country ready to put their shoulder to the wheel to bring progress and prosperity to the country.

What AAP and its leader had to guard against was to harbour

overconfidence, thanks to the fantastic response they received across the country. Partly, the enthusiasm AAP had evoked was because of popular disillusionment with traditional parties and politicians. If Kejriwal were to give the impression that he was as vulnerable as other politicians to the ills of power, even by ostensibly trying to upend the pyramid, it would be the beginning of the end of the brave new world AAP had painted.

THE DYNASTY

The churning process in the Indian polity since the days of Jawaharlal Nehru is divided between the dynasty and others. Even among members of the country's first family, different generations had distinct personalities. After Jawaharlal, daughter Indira was imperious and in many respects became a consummate practitioner of realpolitik. Her favourite younger son Sanjay dabbled in car-making before his attention was diverted by the lure of exercising power without responsibility.

We shall never know the full potential of Sanjay's exercise of power, aside from his harsh family planning methods, compulsorily moving out slum dwellers, and wielding the axe in punishing those crossing his path and rewarding his buddies. In her famous address to a Congress jamboree, Indira said that Sanjay had stolen his elders' thunder. She was preparing Sanjay eventually to succeed her. But fate willed otherwise and the younger son sacrificed his impetuous life while conducting air stunts.

Rajiv Gandhi was a more thoughtful person, an airline pilot to boot, living unostentatiously with his Italian-born wife Sonia and their two children. After her mother-in-law's assassination, Sonia resisted the Congress establishment, installing her husband in the suddenly vacant post. As with so much of the party's first family, history had claimed a role for each successive generation. Rajiv brought some fresh ideas and painted his vision of a modern India and did give a fillip to adopting new technology. But he was soon to be swallowed up in the scandal surrounding the purchase of Bofors field guns. Eventually, he lost an election and while campaigning for the next, lost his life at the hands of a Sri Lankan Tamil Tiger terrorist.

Sonia Gandhi mourned for her husband for a time until she succumbed to two temptations: First, the Congress party, floundering without being led by a member of the dynasty, was drifting. Second, she considered it her duty that, having married into the dynasty, she should prepare her son Rahul for the throne. Having won the 2004 election, Sonia thought it wise to have the loyalist Manmohan Singh take office, in view of the song and dance made by the main opposition BJP about the absurdity of an Italian-born woman taking the highest political office of the land. In a theatrical gesture, Sushma Swaraj, who was to become Narendra Modi's foreign minister, swore to have her head tonsured were Sonia to assume office. Rahul was clearly unprepared to assume the responsibility. And even as the next general election came along in 2009, Rahul, the reluctant politician that he is, was far from ready. Only in the final stages of the Congress party campaign in the 2014 elections, as the underdog, had Rahul shown any perseverance in attempting to do serious political campaigning. The election's result was disastrous for the Congress, with a score card of only 44 seats in the Lok Sabha.

In any assessment of the dynasty, Sonia's contribution to the fortunes of the Congress party will be viewed as a sterling one. Doubtless, she had been imbibing the finer points of playing the political game from her mother-in-law. Indeed, Sonia shared an emotional relationship with Indira unlike the fractious equation the latter had with her other daughter-in-law Maneka, Sanjay's wife. Ironically, both Maneka and her son Varun, have embraced the BJP, the ideological opponent of the Congress.

What about the leaders outside the dynasty who held office? Jawaharlal's immediate successor, Lal Bahadur Shastri, was a transitional figure; he was in office for a very short time. Not counting the parade of prime ministers who came and went in the 1990s with bewildering frequency after the collapse of the first post-Emergency government, Morarji Desai, the veteran Congressman of strong views and a reputation for being rigid, was twice passed over for the top job, given the demands of the first family.

Morarji had little time to display his administrative abilities because the brand new ruling party of many opposition parties, including the Jana Sangh, the earlier avatar of the BJP, was first swallowed up in enumerating the evils of the Emergency and the combine known as the Janata Party was pulling in different directions. The crisis that sank the Janata government was the allegation that the Jana Sangh was inimical to secular values because it was wedded to the philosophy of its mentor, the RSS.

Apart from Manmohan Singh, who was gifted the office of prime minister by Sonia and hence was beholden to her in taking the government's decisions, P.V. Narasimha Rao proved a gifted operator in politics and, unexpectedly being thrust into the job on Rajiv's assassination, made the best of a bad hand. Perhaps his greatest contribution was to lend political support to his then finance minister, Manmohan Singh, to carry out his innovative economic reforms after Jawaharlal's left-of-centre dispensation had reached a dead end.

Rao was a complex man, erudite in several languages, and one who had drunk deep at the fountainhead of ancient Indian wisdom. Like some men of learning, he was convinced of his own superior intellect. It was this overconfidence in his own political abilities that led him to preside over one of the most tragic events of modern Indian history: the destruction of the Babri Masjid at Ayodhya in Uttar Pradesh, then ruled by the BJP, by hordes of party followers under the titular leadership of Lal Krishna Advani while law enforcement officers stood by. The agitation, of course, was in aid of the belief that the sixteenth-century mosque in question was built by Muslim conquerors on the very spot where the Ayodhya temple once stood.

Other non-dynasty prime ministers had their own moments in the sun, but the assumption of office of the first BJP prime minister, Atal Behari Vajpayee, represented a dramatic change. While the BJP prided itself on its own pedigree, Vajpayee was in essence a continuation of an inclusive form of government minted by Jawaharlal, recognizing the ethnic, religious and tribal affiliations of a variety of the country's inhabitants. He had in the process indulged in verbal gymnastics because of the RSS philosophy being narrow-minded.

DEMOCRACY'S FUTURE

The inevitable question posed by developments of recent years is whether the practice of democracy as it has evolved in the country is in danger. Has the accepted idea of India changed? The building blocks of Indian democracy were moulded by the independence struggle and the collective wisdom of exceptional leaders. It was, in essence, an inclusive concept, given the great ethnic, religious and linguistic diversity of the country's inhabitants. In time, such inclusiveness almost became a mantra, repeated ad nauseam by minister and foot soldier alike. Behind it was the belief of the independence leaders that there was no other means of keeping the nation together.

As we have seen, one stream of thought, that of the RSS, collectively the Sangh Parivar, was not in favour of such a concept. The RSS led its charge of India being inhabited by Hindus and even those professing other religions being part of the Hindu ethos and maintained that the country should claim and be proud of its Hindu heritage. Some of the states ruled by the BJP carried their Hindu sensibilities to the extent of banning beef, in view of the traditional reverence given to the cow in the Hindu ethos.

Mahatma Gandhi's assassination represented a major setback to the Sangh Parivar's propagation of its views. But as the horrific act receded in public memory, the RSS revved up its urge to proselytize. The demolition of the Babri Masjid was one event in this chain, but the BJP's success in wresting major states from the Congress gave its mentor, the RSS, the confidence to increase the decibel level of the Hindutva concept it desired to promote.

Against the backdrop of the approaching general elections of 2014 and the stumbles of the second United Progressive Alliance (UPA-II) government and its involvement in a long list of scams, the RSS felt more empowered to proclaim its goal from the housetops. In choosing Narendra Modi as the prime ministerial candidate of the BJP, the RSS felt further emboldened to stake all on his victory. In the meantime, the BJP's brains trust, comprising many non-resident Indians (NRIs), had set about framing an alternative narrative to the idea of India. Its precise formulation is still being debated, but the aim was clear: to substitute the concept of an inclusive India with a dharma regime, one embedded in the beliefs of Hindu religion.

The NRIs residing in the United States, many of whom are American citizens, are some of the most enthusiastic supporters of the Sangh Parivar. Even as their progeny are becoming increasingly Americanized in the famous American melting pot, the older generation often suffers from a feeling of guilt for having abandoned their motherland in search of lucre and compensate this feeling by being more Hindutva-minded than they would otherwise have been. On the other hand, being more attuned to American thinking, they are seeking to convert their narrative into a new Indian theme of exceptionalism in parallel with the American credo.

The impact of this new offensive on the Indian political scene is destabilizing because, given the nature of India, any major overhaul of the idea of India will cause tremors in the body politic. Since this new high decibel campaign is being spearheaded by Modi, known for his efficiency and decisiveness in administration, it bears an autocratic tag. It is no secret that in achieving repeated victories in Gujarat, Modi administered through a few key ministers, political aides and high performing civil servants owing their primary loyalties to him, rather than the state or the country. Besides, in this ends-justifies-means regime, the focus is far from observing democratic norms. The result has been Modi's successful manoeuvre to stall the appointment of a Lokayukta (state-level anti-corruption ombudsman) for a decade and reducing the state legislature's effectiveness.

Indeed, the soaring rhetoric of the Indian Constitution and the love and labour with which it was framed seems a distant memory. The RSS had tried to make its voice heard for a long time but the soil tilled by liberal minds of the independence generation was hostile to the crops it wanted to plant. Given the scale of public disillusionment with the UPA-II, the RSS believes that its moment has arrived. And it can hardly wait to grab it with both hands.

In the process, the practice of democracy has become a punching bag. The country will face a period of adjustment to the new narrative the Sangh Parivar seeks to propagate. In the longer term, the snag is that the only way to govern a varied country is through inclusiveness. The 21-month long internal Emergency offers a salutary lesson. Indira Gandhi split the Congress party twice in order to consolidate power in the face of party bosses who had become too powerful. Her decision to proclaim the Emergency was to survive a legal hurdle to her continuing rule against rising countrywide dissent. But after the shock of an unprecedented regimen and the surface placidity it brought, she was forced to call fresh elections, which she disastrously lost.

It is, however, salutary to remember that after the successor regimes squabbled, there was a succession of stop-gap prime ministers, after which Indira was triumphantly back in power—seemingly the queen of all she surveyed. It was as if the Emergency was an aberration.

MAN BEHIND THE MASK

What is Modi behind the mask, made famous by his brilliant use of it in election campaigns? The most comprehensive biography on him written thus far by Nilanjan Mukhopadhay—*Narendra Modi: The Man, The Times*—tried to get at the man behind the mask. Characteristically, the biographer's interactions with him were abruptly terminated, reminiscent of Karan Thapar's interrupted television interview. One assumes that the author was getting too close to the truth and the subject was unwilling to disclose his real self for fear of besmirching his public persona.

What is beyond controversy is that Modi is an extraordinary man. He was in a sense nurtured in the RSS imbibing for the most part the virtues and myths of the organization. The cult of discipline and steeling of the self for physical fitness suited him. And flowing from the primacy the organization attaches to Hinduism, in the form of Hindutva and otherwise, Modi believes in the mix of history and myths that have come to delineate the RSS creed.

The surprise is not that Modi believes in the myth of head transplants, genetic engineering and space travel being prevalent in ancient India. It is in an RSS apparatchik being an internet geek, a votary of social media such as Twitter and Facebook as a political means of communication.

A typical RSS follower has a crumpled look, except when he gets into khaki shorts for the obligatory morning drill, and mentally lives in the Middle Ages. He is socially conservative, believes that women's rightful place is in the domestic sphere, is uncomfortable talking in English and embraces Hindi or his native tongue. The number of Modi's ministers who answer questions posed to them in English in Hindi on English language television channels is legion. Despite 200 years of British sway over India and the official status English continues to enjoy, most followers of the RSS and the BJP are uncomfortable talking in English. One of the many reasons Arun Jaitley, finance minister, is valued so highly in the new scheme of things is his proficiency in the English language. Modi, in his increasing interactions with world leaders, uses his variety of accented sing-song English to communicate. Indeed, his distinguished predecessor Vajpayee's intonation in English was to copy the tilting pitch of Hindi oratory.

Modi's last stint as Gujarat's chief minister was the training ground for the fulfilment of his ultimate ambition. His accent on no-nonsense development, building infrastructure and providing constant electricity supply, in addition to inviting foreign capital, was a key to his theories of development and progress. Over the years he had developed sufficient influence and confidence to side-line the Sangh Parivar and its shibboleths proving that when it came to exercising power, he could be a pragmatist.

The RSS did not like what it saw but kept quiet because he was winning successive elections in the state along with bringing in development and prosperity to it. With the BJP in good light, the RSS shone too, in Gujarat's reflected glory. When Modi successfully made the transition to the highest political office in the land, the RSS supremo was quick to draw red lines for him. The

RSS *Sarsangchalak*, Mohan Bhagwat, had tolerated his independent ways in Gujarat. His forbearance took a different form with Prime Minister Modi.

Modi's limitations were apparent from his inability to discipline some of his ministers and members of Parliament giving free rein to their extravagant rhetoric. His admonitions were couched in defensive terms and during his meetings with aggrieved Muslims and Christians he usually spoke in general terms of the equality of all Indian citizens, irrespective of faith. It is only more recently towards the end of his first year that he has begun adopting a somewhat more robust approach.

Modi's dilemmas multiplied manifold by the report of the 2011 census made public. It revealed that in the 2001–2011 decade the Muslim population had increased by 14.23 per cent to just over 170 million. Hindus, on the other hand, had dipped to just below 80 per cent. Christians rose by 15.5 per cent remaining at 2.3 per cent of the country's total.

Expectedly, this gave new ammunition to the usual suspects, with Praveen Togadia, the Vishwa Hindu Parishad leader, declaring, 'Hindus must act immediately so that India remains a Hindu majority country or they should get ready for ethnic cleansing...'.

Modi's basic approach is a pragmatic one in resolving problems, despite his own schooling in the myths of Hinduism he presumably still believes in. Perhaps his Gujarati pedigree has helped. Gujaratis, as my four years of schooling in the state showed me, are proficient not only in the art of making money but also in finding practical solutions to problems untrammelled for the most part in getting too involved in ideologies. The teachings of Mahatma Gandhi, the tallest Gujarati, often reduced complex political problems to aphorisms and simple messages. Perhaps it is in the Gujarati gene to put across a message effectively. (There is some merit in the Congress party's complaint that some of the programmes announced by Modi are Congress programmes in a new garb.) In this sense, means are as important as ends.

Modi's pragmatism, it must be noted, is often in conflict with his killer instinct. Hard-hitting electoral campaigning in state elections as prime minister did not faze him. And even as he has learnt to seek the cooperation of the opposition on such issues as the constitutional amendment bill to give effect to the exchange of enclaves with Bangladesh, his land acquisition bill had been tangled in controversies because he was initially inflexible and wanted to have his way, forgetting that he does not have a majority in the Rajya Sabha. His goal was, of course, to open more widely the door to foreign investment and development of agriculture.

In seeking to promote his agenda, he did not give sufficient weight to the fact that land is a very sensitive subject and nearly half of the country's population subsists on land. Apart from irrigated areas in some half of farming land, the farmer relies on rains, which traditionally prove erratic. Indian agriculture requires a massive overhaul. There are too many people living on too little land following traditional methods that yield low productivity. In the end, Modi realized that he had scored an own goal and has been back-paddling in the face of a combined opposition onslaught. His image among farmers has been dented and as a first sop to them, his government announced the start of a television channel, DD Kisan dedicated to farmers and their problems. Finally, he had to accept defeat and withdrew the bill to amend the land acquisition law by desisting from issuing ordinances to keep it alive.

It is none the less ironical that a man steeped in the RSS ethos should have graduated so quickly to become a practitioner of the art of realpolitik. He has many inner conflicts to resolve. Embarrassed by the howls of derision provoked by his Mumbai speech on the veracity of head transplants in ancient India, he chose not to reiterate his belief.

His problem is whether he can let reason and rationality drive out the myths he had learned as true history during the days of his RSS schooling.

A relevant question to be asked right now is—can the Hindu-centric idea of India that Modi learned to believe in negate the idea of India that has been nurtured by the independence generation for more than six decades? The RSS has declared that it wants to change this idea of India. For one thing, it is seeking to promote its own ideas through Smriti Irani and the ministry of human resource development that she heads. Second, the homilies of Bhagwat and his colleagues on overhauling education to rid it of its colonial heritage and introduce Sanskrit at school level are recipes for disaster. A foretaste is offered by Gujarat prescribing school textbooks by Dinanath Batra, a retired school teacher and RSS ideologue. He is convenor of the Shiksha Bachao Andolan Samiti (Save Education Movement). In polite language, Batra's efforts are directed at presenting myths as history.

The fashion is to lump together the embarrassing loud thinking of the Sangh Parivar as fringe elements. The truth is that they do not belong to a fringe but are an important stream of thought in the RSS and its affiliates. They have not kept pace with modern development and technology and are obsessed with the greatness of Hindu culture and civilisation, the universality and wisdom of the epics *Ramayana* and *Mahabharata* and the sayings of the *Gita* that Modi is fond of presenting to foreign heads of state.

An example of Modi's beliefs was his address on the opening of a new wing to a Mumbai hospital. He said: 'We worship Lord Ganesha. There must have been some plastic surgeon at that time who got an elephant's head on the body of a human being and began the practice of plastic surgery.'

While much of Modi's speech was devoted to improving healthcare facilities in modern India, he also dwelled on ancient India's 'capabilities' in several fields at length:

> There must be many areas in which our ancestors made big contributions. Some of these are well recognized. Our ancestors had, at some point, displayed great strengths in space science. What people like Aryabhata had said centuries ago is being recognized by science today. What I mean to say is that we are a country which had these capabilities. We need to regain these.
>
> We can feel proud of what our country achieved in medical science at one point of time. We all read about Karna in the *Mahabharata*. If we think a little more, we realize that the *Mahabharata* says Karna was not born from his mother's womb. This means that genetic science was present at that time. That is why Karna could be born outside his mother's womb.

Modi has publicly articulated such ideas for the first time as prime minister. Earlier, he had written the foreword to a book for school students in Gujarat which maintained that the Hindu God Rama flew the first aeroplane and that stem cell technology was known in ancient India.

The mystery remains. How has such a culture produced a man like Modi?

THE BARGAIN

Modi's upbringing in the RSS and the role the organization played in influencing the BJP's choice for its prime ministerial candidate signified an implicit, if not explicit, bargain. The RSS had picked him from a crowded field because it believed he could be the winner. It was expected that if he did win, he would carry out the RSS agenda.

The RSS priority has always been to mould the minds of the young to inculcate the right (Hindu) values in them through the epics and otherwise, to steel their hearts, resolve and toughen them physically. The organization wants to ensure that what it views as the dark period of Muslim conquests followed by two centuries of British rule is never repeated.

The RSS has evolved its own compendium of myths woven into the golden periods of Hindu kingdoms that ruled the country and venerated the classical language Sanskrit and the gods and goddesses that have come down the ages through folk tales. When BJP leaders pose for television cameras in their home setting, they usually ensure that statues of one or more Hindu gods hover in the background.

Upon winning the general election even more emphatically

than expected, the RSS demanded its pound of flesh and received it in full measure. The person appointed by Modi to the human resources development ministry, which also looks after education and the country's highest institutions of learning, was Smriti Irani, a school leaver who had originally won her spurs as a soap actress in a long-running television serial. A person of substance would have his or her own views on education and the persons to staff various educational institutions. Irani was a blank sheet of paper the RSS could write on.

A sample of what the Sangh Parivar has in store for the young is the following: moral prescriptions from books authored by Dinanath Batra have now become compulsory reading in government schools in Gujarat. On 30 June 2014 the state government issued a circular directing more than 42,000 primary and secondary government schools across the state to make a set of nine books by Batra, translated from Hindi to Gujarati, part of the curriculum's 'supplementary literature'.

Batra's civil suit earlier in 2014 had led to the pulping of American scholar Wendy Doniger's book on Hinduism. He had also sent a legal notice to another publisher about a book on modern Indian history which led the publisher to begin a review of some of its books, including one on sexual violence during riots in Ahmedabad.

The circular issued by the Gujarat State School Textbook Board (GSSTB) reads, 'These books on supplementary literature are aimed at imparting quality education. They will be provided free of cost to all government primary and secondary schools, public libraries and will be also available at GSSTB, Gandhinagar, for individuals interested in these books. These are to be incorporated from this academic session'. On 4 March 2014 Gujarat's education minister Bhupendrasinh Chudasama, released a set of nine books.

On page 59 in *Shikhan nu Bhartiyakaran* (Indianisation of Education), under the chapter 'Samajik Chetna' (social awakening) Batra says, 'Birthdays should be celebrated by shunning the Western culture of blowing candles. Instead, we should follow a purely Indian culture by wearing swadeshi clothes, doing a *havan* (offerings in a consecrated fire) and praying to *ishtadev* (preferred deity), reciting mantras such as Gayatri Mantra, distributing new clothes to the needy, feeding cows, distributing *prasad* (offerings of food) and winding up the day by playing songs produced by Vidya Bharati'.

Page 49 of the book *Tejomay Bharat* (Shining India) reworks India's political map to include some of its neighbours. Batra says, 'Students, how would you go about drawing a map of India? Do you know that countries like Pakistan, Afghanistan, Nepal, Bhutan, Tibet, Bangladesh, Sri Lanka and Burma are part of undivided India? These countries are part of Akhand Bharat'. Another lesson in the chapter, 'Undivided India', reads: 'Undivided India is the truth, divided India is a lie. Division of India is unnatural and it can be united again…'. Batra's hope, encouraged by the RSS fraternity, is that what is prevalent in Gujarat today will be replicated in the whole country.

Irani's lack of institutional education led her to cultivate an air of arrogance in dealing with officers and educationists even as she signed on the dotted RSS line in appointing highly questionable persons in charge of such institutions as the Indian Council of Historical Research, to mention one.

At the same time, Irani tangled with the director of one highly rated Indian Institute of Technology (IIT) and the chairman of another. The director of IIT Delhi, Raghunath K. Shevgaokar, put in his papers to protest against micromanaging by Irani's ministry and the renowned atomic scientist, Anil Kakodkar, chairman of IIT Bombay, absented himself from the selection process for appointing new directors of IITs as a protest against how the interviews were conducted, as if an army of prospective candidates were sought to be appointed in a seemingly fast relay race.

These activities of Smriti Irani and her ministry evoked no response from the Prime Minister's Office, which otherwise is hyperactive in overseeing the work of various ministries. Modi was implicitly acknowledging that he had little leeway in calling the minister to account because she was working under the direction of the RSS.

A second bargain between Modi and the RSS was the number of *sadhus* and other holy men and women in their ochre robes nominated to contest the general election, most of them successfully. The result has been highly embarrassing, if not farcical, with an implicit communal bias as one BJP member of Parliament or another and often junior ministers of Modi's cabinet gave vent to their regressive thoughts. In the process, they often stirred the communal pot, causing fear among members of the large Muslim population and the Christian minority.

A concept honed by the Sangh Parivar is the *ghar vapsi* (return home) movement on the theory that many Hindus were converted to Islam during the days of Muslim conquests and should, in a sense, return home to Hinduism. Similarly, knives in the Parivar are out for Christian missionaries during the more recent colonial period for converting low caste Hindus in particular to their faith.

Some of the gems of advice from BJP members and supporters, including junior ministers, are that each Hindu woman should produce at least four children to balance the rapidly growing Muslim population and the admonition from a junior minister that if people did not like the ban on beef consumption imposed by a number of BJP state governments, they should go to Pakistan.

BJP leaders and supporters often play the communal card in election campaigning in the hope of polarizing voters and consolidating the majority Hindu vote. But the constant stream of anti-Muslim and anti-Christian outbursts has vitiated the atmosphere because followers of the Parivar (the larger BJP family) feel empowered by having a Hindu-oriented government at the national level.

One consequence has been the desecration of many churches and mosques. BJP spokespersons ascribe such acts of vandalism to 'hooligans' and 'miscreants' forgetting that the rhetoric of some of their leaders is an incitement to hurt Muslims and Christians. Even if these acts of vandalism are more criminal than religious in nature, the new verities of political life speak for themselves.

Significantly, during President Barack Obama's otherwise successful visit to Delhi as the chief guest at the Republic Day parade, his parting shot was a homily on the virtues of religious tolerance and inclusiveness to keep India together. He was indirectly highlighting the stark fact that during much of the first year of his rule, Modi had said little to counter the pernicious hate speeches of his followers.

Usually, Modi harps on the virtues of all being equal citizens. On occasion, he grandstands with minority leaders assuring them of equal respect and treatment. It would seem that only after he had completed a full year was he mustering the courage to decry some of the more vicious pronouncements of his party men and women. Perhaps he feels that unlike during his long Gujarat stint, where he successfully sidelined the Sangh Parivar, it is a new ball game at the national level.

CHANGING INDIA

The crucial question that will make or break Narendra Modi and the Sangh Parivar and their legacy is simple. Will the new policies set in motion by Modi's remarkable victory be conducive to the progress of the nation and the welfare of all its citizens? Can the new idea of India being propagated to replace the Mahatma–Nehru philosophy act as a hurdle to keeping the country together?

Sangh Parivar spokespersons say with some justice that the Congress party had often reduced secularism to the concept of using Muslims and other minorities as a vote bank to win elections. But that is no excuse for painting a diverse nation with the saffron brush. Nor does it justify the kind of declarations punctuating the political debate with vicious and downright communal rhetoric pigeonholing minorities, Muslims in particular, as lesser beings who must conform to the Hindu idea of nationhood or be penalized.

As we have seen, these tendentious, if absurd, statements have built up an atmosphere of fear and unease among minorities. At the same time, they have energized sections of the Parivar to wreck churches and mosques. Even if under the RSS credo all permanent residents are considered Hindus, irrespective of their beliefs, such a declaration raises minority hackles. The sense of dismay of minority communities was best expressed by a renowned former police officer and a Christian, Julio Ribeiro, who won plaudits for his role in maintaining peace in several key states in the country.

In the wake of a series of assaults targeting the Christian community, Ribeiro wrote in the *Indian Express* (17 March 2015):

> I am not an Indian any more, at least in the eyes of the proponents of the Hindu Rashtra (nation). Is it coincidence or a well-thought-out plan that the systematic targeting of a small and peaceful community should begin only after the BJP government of Narendra Modi came to power last May?
>
> Many schools, colleges, related establishments that teach skills for jobs have been set up and run by Christians. They are much in demand. Even diehard Hindus have sought admission in such centres of learning and benefited from the commitment and sincerity of Christian teachers....Should they desist from doing such humanitarian work for fear of being so admired and loved that a stray beneficiary converts of his or her own accord? Should only Hindus be permitted to do work that could sway the sentiments of stricken people in need of human love and care?

Ribeiro was given one of the country's highest rewards, the Padma Bhushan, in 1987 for his distinguished service.

However, the Sangh Parivar's bigger targets are Muslims. In Gujarat, Modi's policy after the 2002 killings was to co-opt sections of the community or banish those who suffered by losing their homes and belongings—those who escaped with their lives—to separate areas where they are largely out of view. Modi also empowered a few Muslim businessmen to make money and they collectively serve as his talisman, trotted out on occasion to make his point.

The reactions of Muslims to the large doses of advice they are receiving from the Parivar has varied from offering their organizations' cooperation to the Modi government, seeking shelter behind community leaders or plain defiance from men such as the veteran Hyderabad member of Parliament, Asaduddin Owaisi, president of All-India Majlis-e-Ittehad-ul Muslimeen (MIM). Instead of de-emphasizing his religious affiliation, he flaunts it by arriving at public events featuring him as a speaker more than an hour late because he has to perform his evening *namaz* (prayers) first.

Owaisi has had several brushes with the law and spent short periods in jail. His in-your-face manner has won him many admirers in his community and alarmed the Samajwadi Party of Uttar Pradesh, which relies for its electoral fortunes on the support it receives from a large Muslim electorate. The MIM is spreading its wings in geographically distant Uttar Pradesh from its base in Hyderabad. Instead of shying away from controversies, Owaisi courts them.

Indian Muslims are more than 172 million strong and cannot be wished away. In a sense, the manner of the bloody partition of the subcontinent is a cross the people of the two countries must bear. In philosophical and ideological terms, it was simpler for Pakistanis because they wanted their new state to comprise Muslim-majority areas. Ironically, religion alone proved insufficient to keep the two wings of the new nation state together.

For Indians proclaiming to retain the new truncated nation's secularism as a creed, it was harder to convince people that despite the religion-based division, they should stay secular. It was the moral authority of Nehru and his colleagues that kept the new nation on an even keel. But the other view was strikingly brought home to India and the world by the assassin of Gandhi following his own belief system.

Modi's dilemma is at two levels. As he has himself confessed, he has imbibed the beliefs of the RSS and still believes in the myths he digested at a young impressionable age. At the same time, as he has shown during his long stint in Gujarat, he is pragmatic enough to keep his beliefs to one side to rule as an effective administrator. But as he is discovering each day, the nation is not Gujarat, as his surrender to the RSS on the nation's educational policies and appointments to important historical and research organizations reveals.

A major controversy was in relation to the appointment of an actor in a television serial based on the epic *Mahabharata* and a BJP member, Gajendra Chauhan, as chairman of the reputed Film and Television Institute of India (FTII) in Pune. The students rebelled, held demonstrations and went on strike. They were particularly sore that a man they portrayed as a party hack had been appointed disregarding famed film directors on the short list. The BJP government has a fatal attraction for television actors supporting the party. Witness the cabinet post given to the political novice and soap actress Smriti Irani.

The second problem is the veto power the RSS tends to exercise over the prime minister's decisions even outside the educational sphere. There must come a time when Modi will have to cry halt to being overruled or forfeit the trust of the nation. It will not be too long before such a situation will arise.

JAI YOGA

Narendra Modi helped persuade the United Nations to declare a World Yoga Day, and when it agreed to do so on 21 June every year, the death anniversary of the first supreme leader of the RSS, Keshav Baliram Hedgewar, he was in the seventh heaven. Yoga, which has its roots in Buddhism and Hinduism, serves several of the prime minister's purposes. It pleases his mentors in the RSS and secures an international imprimatur the Sangh Parivar and other Indians so ardently desire. For the Sangh Parivar, it seemingly validates the glories of ancient India for the amazing kinds of things they believe Indians were capable of.

Modi, himself a yoga practitioner, led a mass yoga performance on the first World Yoga Day on the vast expanse of India Gate, in the presence of Baba Ramdev, the nearest thing to an official yoga adviser to the BJP government. It was not lost on the people that the venue is the setting for the annual Republic Day military parade. Yoga performances were repeated elsewhere across the country and in some international cities around the world, including New York. The RSS was riding high because it had firmly wrapped up yoga not only in the colours of Hinduism but also in saffron hues and the mast of nationalism. In other words, yoga became the ultimate symbol of India's greatness. An RSS spokesman, Manmohan Vaidya, proudly declared, 'By celebrating yoga on a mass scale we are validating our glorious past'. Excitement was running high among RSS functionaries and workers alike. Ram Madhav, one of the BJP's senior general secretaries, goofed by pointing to the absence of the country's Muslim vice-president, Hamid Ansari, from the mass yoga show in Delhi. A quick retort from the vice-president's office said he was not invited. As BJP functionaries tried to hide their blushes, it was revealed that since Modi was the principal guest and the vice-president ranked higher in protocol, he had indeed not been invited.

On the other hand, yoga has become a world brand and a multi-billion dollar industry flourishing in many countries, particularly in the United States. Its religious roots have posed problems in many countries in the form of such symbolisms as the *surya namaskar*, invocation to the Hindu Sun God. Kamal Farooqui, a member of the All India Muslim Personal Law Board, said in a radio interview that 'yoga is not the only form of exercise' and by promoting yoga, the BJP was trying to push its Hindu agenda.

Even more pointedly, Maulana Muhammad Wali Rahmani, the working general secretary of the board, asked Muslim organizations, institutions and imams of mosques to close ranks against Hindutva forces. He decried the growing influence of 'Brahmin dharma and Vedic culture [that] are out to harm Islamic beliefs by all means'. Muslims in India and elsewhere have particularly objected to the salutation earning the ire of the BJP member of Parliament Yogi Adityanath saying critics should 'drown in the sea'. Significantly, Modi did not practise the *surya namaskar* at the New Delhi extravaganza. Two other critical comments give the texture of the Indian debate. According to the British Broadcasting Corporation, Ajaz Ashraf, a commentator, said Modi's celebration 'is a mix of cultural nationalism, commercialization and subtle coercion'. And historian Dilip Simeon has derided 'the deceitful polemic of yoga'.

Other countries have found the Hindu religious underpinning of yoga troubling. Some states in Malaysia have prohibited it while others allow it without chanting and meditation, a course Indonesia, the world's largest Muslim-majority country, has also followed. Indeed, yoga is repackaged in the United States, with some schools in California replacing Sanskrit names with commonly used English words. A United States court has ruled that while the roots of yoga were religious, a modified form of hatha yoga, the commonly practiced form, was kosher.

Significantly, many Muslim and Jewish practitioners and teachers of yoga find yoga poses and meditation of immense value and say that there was nothing in them inimical to their faiths. Meditation in particular, some suggest, helped bring them closer to their gods. In this category are some practitioners and teachers of yoga in Iran.

I received three SMSs on my mobile telephone on three successive days starting Friday before the Sunday climax at India Gate. They were from the newly-minted Ayush ministry of the Indian government that looks after yoga. They said: 'Practice (using the American spelling) yoga. It can make you feel active, energetic and positive. Live life to its full potential; Rejuvenate with Yoga. It enriches the consciousness and makes one feel alert, aware and active.'

Opposition leaders panned the event as an image-building exercise for Modi, with one leader taking aim at the corpulent figure of BJP president Amit Shah and other veteran party leaders.

KEJRIWAL'S TRANSFORMATION

Arvind Kejriwal's transformation from an anti-corruption advocate and street fighter to a shrewd hard-boiled politician is a remarkable phenomenon in Indian politics, without parallel. Politicians in the country, perhaps more than in other democracies, have proved fickle in their political affiliations and laws have had to be enacted to curb such opportunism, with somewhat limited results.

But never before has an outsider riding on the shoulders of a non-party crusader come to form his own political party, tellingly named the Aam Aadmi Party (AAP, Common Man's Party) to win enough seats in the Delhi assembly elections to form a government (with Congress support) in 2013 on the strength of popular acclaim for his idealistic goals and to throw in the towel after a little over a month.

The setting for the re-election, when finally called in February 2015 was ideal for Kejriwal with his promise to complete his five-year term, if elected. And there were his conscience keepers in the shape of Yogendra Yadav and Prashant Bhushan to lend him the moral high ground over the BJP and the Congress.

Delhi's voters took Kejriwal and his main supporters at their word and rallied splendidly to give AAP an unprecedented sweep in an avalanche that reduced the BJP to three seats in a house of 70, with the Congress scoring a duck.

Kejriwal was a changed man. He was not only home and dry but in the gravy for five years. With that kind of majority, he had no fear of defections. And he set about changing his party even while taking a medical sabbatical for his respiratory problems. His first task was to cast away his conscience keepers, who kept reminding him about the moral basis of his victory. Both Yadav and Bhushan considered themselves the leader's equal, for good reasons. Kejriwal had his hatchet men initiate the job of removing them while he recuperated in a southern medical facility.

Kejriwal had other scores to settle. No other political leader after the independence generation has received the encouragement he did from an eager media, particularly from television channels. Sometimes, it seemed that media were fighting his battles, eager to support someone who was genuinely interested in people's problems after the demise of the independence generation.

An otherwise endearing trait of Kejriwal is that he is bold in taking decisions. And he seems to have come to the conclusion that expelling his conscience keepers was only the first step to have the field all to himself to govern. There were the other conscience keepers, media, who would judge him by his faithfulness to his promises. And he knew their power by their ability to make him the victor.

Having earmarked media as his next enemy, he chose to act, accusing them of taking *supari* (contract) to seek to finish AAP. And taking his battle cry further, he issued a directive to his administration officials to recommend filing criminal defamation cases against some media entities. The Supreme Court stayed this directive while pointing out the contradiction in his own appeal in a defamation case, suggesting that such offences should not carry the criminal tag.

At its heart, Kejriwal's problem is simple. After having won a famous victory, he wanted to function as any shrewd successful politician practises his craft. How then does he fight his future battles with a nagging media yapping at his heels? If he holds on to his original moral high ground, he would be handicapped in dealing with traditional politicians and cannot hope to fulfil his greater ambitions.

Perhaps unwittingly, he gave the game away by suggesting that 'good people' should take on the job of starting newspapers and television channels to report facts as they are—a task in which his administration would help. It is difficult to think of a more transparent attempt at starting a pro-government media outlet in the tried Communist fashion.

Kejriwal's support has eroded. Many AAP followers have resigned, and the generous London soul who had gifted him the Maruti Suzuki WagonR hatchback has asked to have his car back. Indeed, the speed of Kejriwal's farewell to his ideals was audacious.

What then lies in store for Kejriwal and the shattered dreams of all those taken in by the new politics he was supposed to herald in the country? The AAP leader probably believes that his crushing majority in the Delhi assembly makes him immune to the evil of defection. Second, in common with the well-established Communist practice, he will seek to connect directly with the people over the heads of media, lacing his actions with dollops of populist measures. His party's budget has allotted a generous amount of money for publicity. A sampling of his television commercials has a common theme: greater glory for Kejriwal and his government, tagged as such, not given the appellation of the AAP government.

To muddy the waters further for AAP, his law minister, Jitender Singh Tomar, was arrested on the charge of faking his law degree, and while one might quibble over the manner or propriety of the arrest, the AAP minister's record does not enhance the party's credentials. Quick on the heels of Tomar's predicament was a physical assault charge made by the wife of another prominent AAP member, Somnath Bharti. Another AAP member of the Delhi legislative assembly was charged with making a land deal on the basis of forged papers and was temporarily sent to jail. Charges were reportedly pending in the case of several more members of the Delhi assembly, including another one reportedly sporting a false degree.

Popular disillusion with Kejriwal's new avatar seems to be spreading and if this sense of betrayal takes hold, there can come a time when his seemingly rock solid majority will begin to erode.

Obviously, many people who voted for him did so in the belief that here at last was a man who would purify the well of Indian politics heralding a vanished sense of idealism to revive the halcyon days of the giants of the independence movement.

Despite speculation, it is not easy for Kejriwal's newly disillusioned critics to form a new party. The AAP's birth took place against the backdrop of the Anna Hazare movement on the strength of the good work done by him in his hometown in Maharashtra before taking it to the national level.

The political atmosphere was thick with the odour of a litany of scams in the second term of the United Progressive Alliance government. The national mood was receptive to a man acting in the Gandhian tradition of selfless service. While Hazare packed his bags and went home, Kejriwal cashed in on the movement.

The AAP leader was never in doubt on two points. First, he had to stamp his authority on the baby party. Second, while the morality stick was good to wave, the hard reality of playing politics had to take priority.

Yogendra Yadav and Prashant Bhushan, with their persistent admonitions and waving the flag of morality, had simply become too distracting and inconvenient for Kejriwal's plan to rule his fledgling party with an iron hand. He had had a taste of their mettle by their objecting to some of the tainted candidates fielded by the party and they had raised questions about large dubious donations.

Kejriwal thus came to the conclusion that nothing short of a purge of the two from the political affairs committee would do. And he set about it in the hoary tradition of Indian political culture pioneered by the Congress party and followed by all others. First, seek their resignation while airing Yadav's clandestinely taped conversation with a journalist to embarrass him and then offer inconsequential posts to sideline them.

When every trick failed, they were voted out in the executive by a surprisingly narrow 11 to 8 margin. True to the accepted political tradition, Kejriwal absented himself with the plausible excuse of undergoing treatment while sending in his own resignation as party convener, predictably rejected.

Kejriwal won a victory at great cost. Its quantum remains to be determined. The plan did not run to script because neither of the gadflies had an ulterior motive in raising the questions they did. They sought to keep AAP on the straight and narrow: moral imperatives that had persuaded them and so many others to support a party seeking higher moral ground. The immense response it got in Delhi was due to the electors' belief that here was a new party of leaders with conviction who wanted to change the way politics was played.

As far as most supporters were concerned, the let-down was tremendous. While some compromises are necessary in politics as in life, the duplication of the traditional deviousness practised by Kejriwal's henchmen was breathtaking. The Delhi chief minister might undertake an act of showmanship to try to surmount his huge embarrassment, but he would find it difficult to regain trust.

Perhaps the questioning duo was being unrealistic in trying to keep AAP to a high moral benchmark. Perhaps it also became a question of Kejriwal's *amour propre*, of men of an intellectual standing challenging his actions in the party. Perhaps the leader who abandoned Anna Hazare's movement to start a political party felt that only as an unchallenged leader could he deliver on his promises.

By their very nature, these are assumptions, but the crisis in AAP posed larger questions. Can a party that sought to give a new direction to Indian political culture survive the body blow that has been dealt it? How will Kejriwal convince his bewildered supporters that he remains sincere in fulfilling his promises? Has he indeed misjudged his two critics into believing that they can be tackled through traditional methods of placating or expelling them?

These are portentous questions that go to the heart of the rationale for a new party. Judging by the number of defections to the BJP after its impressive victory in the Lok Sabha elections last year, politicians gravitate towards power, especially when the future of the losing party seems bleak. To give one example of horse-trading, we all know how P.V. Narasimha Rao converted his minority government at the centre into a majority dispensation.

The shock over how the AAP crisis was managed was in the tawdry nature of the tricks that were played upon the dissenting duo by Kejriwal loyalists. They hopelessly misread the dissenters who were not raising objections for their own aggrandizement, but were highlighting the nature of the compromises made in winning the Delhi elections.

Kejriwal's stance of being above the conflict by absenting himself from the executive meeting and sending in his own resignation are old tricks in the political game. It is worth noting, however, that in a vainglorious move, he divested himself of all portfolios in the newly-formed Delhi ministry so that he remained the monarch of all he surveyed.

The tragedy for those who voted for AAP in Delhi—and millions more across the country cheering it—is that the melodrama that played out in the executive committee came so soon after its unprecedented triumph.

Whatever the future holds for AAP, the party witnessed its watershed moment. The party on the hill tottered and Kejriwal's task now was how to rescue it from the dirty politics played in his name and presumably under his direction. There would be little profit in dissembling to suggest that he was unaware of what was being enacted.

Many AAP supporters and the wider public will wonder whether they had again backed the wrong horse. By turning the party's back on two of its most illustrious founder members, it betrayed the trust of many.

BUILDING NEW ICONS

Modi's zeal in centralizing power has taken him to a direct fight with the judiciary by proposing a new formula, a National Judicial Appointments Commission (NJAC), for appointment of judges to the Supreme Court and high courts to replace the existing collegial system under the Chief Justice of India (CJI).

Constitutionally, the President (that is the executive) was the authority for appointing judges to the Supreme Court and high courts in consultation with the CJI, but Ashoke Kumar Sen, law minister in Jawaharlal Nehru's cabinet said the CJI knew best and his word should be honoured.

As convincingly argued by the senior advocate, Fali S. Nariman, before the Supreme Court, this blissful state of real judicial independence lasted some 45 years. According to the NJAC formulation, the CJI and two fellow judges could be overruled by two 'eminent persons' on the committee. Judging by the choice of eminent persons appointed by the Modi government to important positions, the country would have little trust in such appointments. And the judiciary is fighting against the new perceived attack on judicial independence.

Of greater political import are the important convulsions taking place in the BJP against Modi's style of functioning. Veteran BJP leader Lal Krishna Advani's unhappiness has been recorded. It did not take a Sherlock Holmes to decipher that Advani was aiming his barbs at Modi, who had displaced him as the BJP's prime ministerial candidate. Indeed, at that time he had made his displeasure clear by resigning from all party posts before reconsidering his move.

Apart from voicing his own sense of grievance, Advani was making a larger point, that Modi's highly personalized and centralized method of governance was inimical to the interests of the BJP and the country at large.

However, Modi is playing a bigger game by seeking to build a new set of icons for the alternative view of India that he has been promoting. He has no inhibitions in plundering the Congress party with abandon. He had initially chosen to appropriate the Mahatma for his own reform agenda. As icons go, he was simply too important to ignore. But his most daring coup has been virtually to adopt the Congress leader and Nehru's deputy prime minister and India's first home minister, Sardar Vallabhbhai Patel, as a true symbol for what he stands for.

There are several reasons for Modi to go for the Sardar as his party's new mascot. He is a fellow Gujarati and was justly renowned for his contribution in bringing in almost all princely states, technically independent to decide their future on Indian independence, into the fold of the newly independent country. The two that did not agree were taken by force. He was also a more homespun politician and unlike Nehru, had few illusions about China and made his views known to the then prime minister.

Modi proposed that a statue of the Sardar, higher than New York's Statue of Liberty, be installed in Gujarat. Although the BJP's last budget made a provision for it, the party has appealed for donations to make the ambitious project a reality. Modi, of course, has a partiality for showmanship and prefers the grand gesture to make his point.

In parallel, the new dispensation is seeking to diminish the dynasty's role in the making of India. It has singled out P.V. Narasimha Rao for honour in the belief that he was not given his due because he was not accommodated in Delhi's home for the good and the great at the Rajghat site.

Thus the alternative history of India is sought to be buttressed by leaders more to Modi's taste, in addition to gods and goddesses and the mythological heroes of the epics. The Modi-appointed chairperson of the Indian Council of Historical Research, Y. Sudershan Rao, is concerned that 'leftist historians' did not accept that Lord Ram was born in Ayodhya where the Babri Masjid was destroyed under the benediction of Advani when he led his supporters to the town.

The learned Rao told a seminar organized by an RSS-linked organization at the National Museum in New Delhi, 'I went to Ayodhya. Just walk through the streets—you will get the feeling of living in *Ramayana* times...I had this feeling. You can't call it a myth, that's my experience'. For the RSS and many of its supporters, myth is history and history is myth. How will the country's future historians emerge out of this tunnel vision?

ADVANI TO THE FORE

With Atal Behari Vajpayee incapacitated, Lal Krishna Advani remains the rare remaining physical link with the founders of the parent and mentor organizations that represent what has evolved into the Sangh Parivar. It is worth recalling that at one time he represented the hard face of Hindutva, had led the controversial *rath yatra* and was, to put it politely, a spectator to the destruction of the Babri mosque. He was later to apologise for his supporters' vandalism, which seemed to have been a planned affair at several levels.

Perhaps his stint in the first Janata government gave him a new awareness of the complexities of governing a country like India. Perhaps he has evolved and realized the handicaps in taking a narrow view of the country through Hindu eyes alone, particularly in unsuccessfully seeking the prime minister's office in 2009. It is a matter of historical record that he was frustrated by Modi in making a second attempt. Modi had convinced the RSS that he was the man who could bring home the elusive victory.

Nobody in the BJP could quarrel with Modi after his famous victory. Advani receded to the background—until the sheen began to wear off the Teflon prime minister who could do no wrong. And with the 40th anniversary of the imposition of the Emergency looming, he granted a full-length interview to the *Indian Express* (25 June 2015).

Advani went for the jugular: 'I don't think anything has been done [since the Emergency] that gives me the assurance that civil liberties will not be suspended or destroyed again. Not at all...Of course, no one can do it easily...But that it cannot happen again, I will not say that, it could be that fundamental liberties are curtailed again'.

The opposition rejoiced. Even the Congress, whose leader had imposed the Emergency, joined in the chorus. Advani had chosen the timing well. The BJP tried to put a brave face on it, but embarrassment among the party's leaders was obvious. Narendra Modi's penchant for decisiveness could be made to look authoritarian, his centralisation of power in the Prime Minister's Office was a byword. There are always winners and losers in any new party dispensation and those on the losing side rejoiced.

And with other controversies swirling around the external affairs minister, Sushma Swaraj, and the BJP chief minister of Rajasthan state, Vasundhara Raje Scindia, over their role in helping the former cricket czar Lalit Modi, a fugitive from Indian justice, Advani again waded in.

Just when Narendra Modi and his party and supporters were congratulating themselves on completing one year of what they touted as scam-free rule, the bomb had exploded. It was in the deceptive shape of a 'humanitarian gesture'. Swaraj was in the centre of the storm, which also singed Vasundhara Raje.

In basic terms, the issue was simple. Should Swaraj in her official capacity have helped Lalit Modi in obtaining British official documents for travel? He was residing in London, his Indian passport had been seized (until restored by a high court order) and he wanted to be in Portugal for his wife's cancer surgery.

The report of Lalit Modi's adventures was broken by London's *Sunday Times* and the Indian media, in hot pursuit, chased him to

Montenegro, with the India Today television channel scoring a scoop. Putting most of the pieces together in the jigsaw puzzle, it presented a sorry picture of wheeling and dealing by a consummate operator involving Keith Vaz, British member of Parliament, and the families of Swaraj and Scindia.

What was equally clear was that Swaraj was very unwise in acting as she did. How far her judgement was influenced by her family's long association with Lalit Modi is a matter of conjecture. But her daughter was working on the cricket boss's legal team and her husband had been on his legal team for more than 20 years and had sought a favour from him for the admission of a nephew to a British university.

Scindia was compromised by her close ties with Lalit Modi and his ailing wife, the cricket czar's reported investment in her son's company and her affidavit in support of the besieged Indian as long as her intervention was kept secret. Scindia had been family friends of the Modis of long standing.

For the opposition parties, led by the Congress, the drama, played out on 24-hour television, was a welcome gift to score points at a self-righteous ruling party that was feasting on the scams that seemed to define the United Progressive Alliance government, Mark II. Lalit Modi's belligerent-sounding defence of his actions in the interview he gave Rajdeep Sardesai in Montenegro did not help Swaraj's cause. Rather, it reinforced the impression of a buccaneer ready to take on the Indian government and the world. It also nullified the impression his lawyer made in Mumbai to explain his client's point of view.

The opposition went for the obvious contradictions in the official story, with Arun Jaitley, finance minister, fielding for his colleague in distress. How could Swaraj go out of her way by telling British officials that her government would not object to their granting Lalit Modi United Kingdom travel papers?

A host of other questions arose. Why could New Delhi not have granted him temporary Indian papers to enable him to visit his sick wife in Portugal and forced him to return home to face the charges? The previous government had told London that bilateral relations would be affected if Modi were granted travel privileges. Swaraj therefore played a crucial role in enabling him to travel out of London, and apart from visiting his wife, participate in a family wedding and holiday in Montenegro, among other tourist spots.

Swaraj was living on borrowed time. The opposition was calling for the resignation of Vasundhara Raje Scindia. The reported financial element in Modi's relationship with the Scindia family was problematic.

These developments had a wider significance inasmuch as Prime Minister Narendra Modi's thrust in fighting corruption would be less effective, given the influence of a man under investigation for malpractices exercising the hold he apparently had on two important BJP leaders, apart from other leaders across parties. Also, the cloak of probity the national BJP leadership wore so self-consciously had developed holes.

The Congress had the opportunity to take on the Modi government. But it had a very long road to travel, with Rahul Gandhi still having to prove his ability to lead. He seemed stuck in the felicitous phrase 'suit-boot government' to criticize BJP rule on all occasions.

Despite the new broom the prime minister had chosen, literally and metaphorically, to clear the cobwebs of the country's administrative structure, it could only be the beginning of a long process. Most BJP leaders have been nurtured in the political ethos that evolved over the decades. The exceptions are the RSS workers seconded to the BJP with an ideological agenda, the prime minister himself being one of them.

The BJP has of course made many compromises in government formation at the centre and in the states to field winnable candidates, whatever their deficiencies. But Swaraj's case presented another kind of problem for the prime minister. She was one of the aspirants to the prime minister's *gaddi* (chair) after the forced retirement of Advani. Once Modi was chosen, she had to be given a senior cabinet position. After winning the election, he had the felicitous idea of giving her the external affairs portfolio. Being the activist he proved to be in the foreign policy field, she had been boxed in.

Even as Modi sought to touch base with the larger public by his programme on All India Radio titled *Mann Ki Baat* (heart-felt conversation), Advani injected his own *mann ki baat*. With two senior BJP leaders under scrutiny, the former deputy prime minister of India said in an interview that credibility was essential and politicians must live up to the trust of the voters. Nudging the two leaders further, he said he had no regrets in resigning from the Lok Sabha in 1996 after his name was linked to a scandal. He added: 'I don't have any regrets that I couldn't contest the election for two years. The decision to quit was mine.'

Misfortunes, they say, never come alone. Topping these embarrassments was the growing dimension of the Vyapam scandal, a mind-boggling exam cheating and recruitment scam, in Madhya Pradesh state ruled by the BJP putting the chief minister, Shivraj Singh Chouhan, under scrutiny. What was macabre was the mysterious deaths of more than 40 people connected with it in some way, including a television reporter who went to investigate, the dean of the state medical college and a new woman police recruit.

In response to petitions, the Supreme Court took matters in its own hand by ordering a federal Central Bureau of Investigation (CBI) probe into the gargantuan scandal and the unexplained deaths. Indeed, in desperation, Chouhan had agreed to a CBI investigation to save his skin. The writing on the wall was staring him in the face. How could he let a scandal of such proportions run its course for years under his stewardship?

Advani conceives himself as something of a conscience keeper for the BJP. At the same time, he is keeping himself relevant in a party in which he no longer has an effective role. And he gives sustenance to the murmurs of dissent in the party.

A PARADOX

There is little doubt that Narendra Modi wants to leave his imprint on India's history. He has the stamina, the will power and administrative and political skills to benefit the country in its development and modernisation. Equally, he has immense problems and challenges to confront and, above all, the sum total of his own beliefs which take him to a world of fantasy he has been nurtured on.

Modi is a paradox in many ways. By all accounts, he believes in the magic of ancient India, not merely in the wisdom the sages left us in the form of the epics *Ramayana* and *Mahabharata* but also in the celestial words of the *Gita*. His world encompasses an ancient world of many modern miracles.

Admittedly, these myths were part of his upbringing from a young age in the lap of the possessive world of the RSS. The organization, in the Indian idiom, was both mother and father to him. And yet this diligent impressionable young man, who left his wife and family to follow the RSS command, not only learned the finer points of the political game but also acquired an obsessive interest in communication technology and used it to telling effect in his political career in campaigning and directly communicating with the people.

This paradox raises a host of questions. It came as something of a shock that Modi was willing to sacrifice the entire field of education from the primary level to the highest institutes to please the RSS and appoint as its head a school leaver to show his contempt for the entire intellectual community. The kind of absurdities that have been introduced in Gujarat schools is beyond belief. Yet Modi does not spare a thought for the consequences. And reputed institutes of technology and administration are now sought to be smothered in the government's embrace. The symbolism of Baba Ramdev dispensing his wisdom at the Indian Institute of Technology (IIT) Delhi says it all. And RSS voices are being raised to paint IITs as elitist and in need of repair by imparting doses of Hindutva. The RSS weekly, *Organiser*, has thought it fit to denigrate the IITs, taken by many as the first shot across its bow.

Modi likes to consider himself a modernizer and yet he tries to connect to it with the help of myths. One does not associate modernity with an average RSS apparatchik, however sterling he might be in other respects. Modi has an innate talent for public speaking in his native Gujarati and in Hindi and knows how to sway audiences. When he tries to speak in English for an international audience, the effect is somewhat different. Although he might miss nuances in the language, he makes himself well understood.

Was it then his Gujarati genes that helped him connect with modern communication to advantage? For a politician who likes to retain all the aces, social media have the great advantage of a one-way communication, with no hard questions asked of him. It is easier to ignore rude tweets.

In administration Modi has made good governance his theme song and proudly flaunts his record of economic development and prosperity, as in the case of Gujarat. The state however has a poor record in health and social welfare and ranks low in the pecking order. And the future he envisages for the country is a narrow and warped one, guided as it is by the myths taught him and an overall resentment of the rest of the world he shares with the RSS for having humiliated his great land. Therefore, a United Nations-sanctioned World Yoga Day has had such great resonance for Modi and the RSS.

Modi's Hindu view of India and the world presents problems in the twenty-first century. It vitiates the inter-communal atmosphere stoked nearly every day by his Parivar followers in the unfortunate legacy of the subcontinent's bloody Partition that has led to three major wars between India and Pakistan. And majoritarianism is not the way to seek communal harmony in the country.

Has Modi considered the costs of polluting education at various levels, starting with schools to the highest institutions of learning? If this is the price Modi is willing to pay for RSS support, whatever his own beliefs, is the cost sustainable?

Modi's accession to power was broadly welcomed because the Congress-led coalition had had its day. It was tired and afflicted with the handicap of having a prime minister beholden to his party president for gifting him the office. Here was a new prime minister who seemed his own boss, was decisive and had the will power to enforce decisions.

Soon it came to pass that Modi had a big ego and was limited in his ken by his own upbringing in the RSS and although he could, on occasion set aside his prejudices to innovate and communicate with the people, his minders in the mentor organization had left him little room for sensible educational reforms and a clear-headed view of history.

The larger question on the horizon is becoming more compelling. Is the Hindutva concept viable? The ideas that evolved into what became the RSS were insurrectionary in nature. During much of the early decades of independent India, the Sangh Parivar was an outsider looking in. Its electoral triumphs began in the states and it built up steam as Congress fortunes dipped. The Vajpayee government in Delhi was in a sense a continuation of the Nehruvian enterprise, with the leader hiding behind the limitations of a coalition dispensation and Vajpayee's way with words was such that he was able to reconcile the contradictions of being an RSS person and a moderate.

Modi's dilemma is that he has an overall majority in the Lok Sabha and is a very different person from Vajpayee. He has therefore to face the stark choice of a deeply convinced RSS man holding the highest executive office in the land called upon by his mentors to deliver on his promises. And he has a Hindu-majority country with more than 172 million Muslims, in addition to other important minorities, in which to establish his Hindutva credentials.

For more than a few of Sangh Parivar followers, it has been a field day for pronouncing their edicts steeped in clothes of anti-Muslim and anti-Christian hues. On occasion, Modi is forced to pronounce Olympian-sounding edicts on citizen rights and equality but is powerless to act against offenders, be they, members of Parliament or mere party members.

The central paradox is obvious. India cannot be run as the obverse side of the Islamic State or caliphate. What direction will Modi take to translate the RSS concept of the Golden Age into practice? He still has the excuse of being a minority in the Rajya Sabha in order to prevaricate. The choice is stark. Is he willing to give up his own and the Parivar's sacred beliefs to govern the country effectively, even after packing research and historical organizations with RSS men? Will Modi's concept of Hindu India fly?

THE FUTURE

Where does the Modi dispensation and India go from here? The Prime Minister is ensconced for the rest of his five-year term and is doubtless looking forward to repeating the exercise. There is a lot going for him if he grasps his opportunities and steers clear of fantasies learned in the lap of the RSS and is able to insulate the area of administration from his minders in the mentor organization. There lies the rub.

As one would expect from a showman of his abilities, a hagiography is quickly building up in the number of books on him rolling off the presses. Some are totally partisan while others try to observe a measure of balance, but all of them deal with the fateful events of 2002 in Gujarat shortly after he assumed the office of chief minister. As the man on the spot, Kingshuk Nag had the following to say in his book *The NaMo Story: A Political Life*: 'Having witnessed the riots closely, I can say with authority that any government that showed such indifference in continuing the carnage elsewhere in the country would have been dismissed immediately and the state put under President's rule'.

Nag elaborates: 'Though he should have tried hard to quell the riots, perhaps Modi may have believed that trying to do so would result in his getting upstaged. So, instead of trying to control the riots, he stood by as a passive spectator. His critics, however, allege that he was more than just that'.

The Special Investigation Team gave Modi a clean chit saying there was no 'prosecutable evidence' to try him.

On the other side, Modi made a coup with the British author Andy Marino who was given royal treatment in Gujarat and could boast of his frank conversations with the chief minister beyond any granted to a journalist or author. As a long-time foreign correspondent around the world, I am familiar with a technique employed by leaders in difficulty because a foreigner, however diligent, can never be as knowledgeable as a native and can be influenced by access to the top and ostensible shared confidences.

And Marino delivered handsomely in his book *Narendra Modi: A Political Biography*. He writes after delivering the verdict:

> I can say with some certainty that Modi is clinical but not cold. He has a calm about him that is at odds with the fierce persona he exhibits at public rallies.
>
> Although the deaths occurred during his tenure and although he must carry the remorse for the rest of his life, the facts show that Modi did not want them to happen, did not help them to happen, and did everything in his power as quickly as he could to stop them happening. It is irrelevant to him that he performed better than any Congress chief minister.

As outlined in the first chapter, Modi has never apologized for the 2002 riots. The nearest he came to an apology was in an interview he gave to Shahid Siddiqui, editor and publisher of the Urdu weekly *Nai Duniya* with a mainly Muslim readership, in July 2012. Modi said: 'What is the point in apologizing now? I took full responsibility for what happened during that time, expressed sorrow and apologized.

Please check what I said in 2002 after the riots. Now you should write that you [media] have been doing injustice to me for the past 10 years. You should now apologise to Modi'.

An area of governance staring the country in the face is the country's education policy farmed out to the RSS, with results we are we are witnessing every day. There are frequent admonitions from the Sangh Parivar on how wrong the current system is and the outlandish ideas promoted by the new purveyors of education and research, which could be entertaining if they were not so tragic for the future of the young generation.

A second problem is the conflict within Modi himself. As I have illustrated in earlier chapters, he still seems to believe the myths he has learnt in his earlier avatar as a humble RSS worker. While he was pragmatic enough as Gujarat's chief minister to set aside his own beliefs to further the state's development and seek quick technology-aided solutions, he has met a bigger roadblock in his role as the country's prime minister. How far he will surrender to the RSS worldview remains to be seen. Ironically, the RSS did not object to the most technology-driven general election campaign India has ever seen because it was for the cause of ensuring a victory.

Modi's autocratic character has been widely commented upon and, according to Ullekh NP in his book *War Room: The People, Tactics and Technology Behind Narendra Modi's 2014 Win*, 'Modi never forgave or forgot his enemies'. Another trait that has attracted public attention is his tendency to glorify himself, as is apparent from his portraits appearing in newspapers and on hoardings across Gujarat—later in large parts of the country. He still has to live down his monogrammed pinstripe suit.

Modi's clearest answer in justifying this trait was given to Uday Mahurkar in *Centrestage: Inside the Narendra Modi Model of Governance*. Confronting him on his hunger for publicity, Modi shot back: 'Why should I not when I am doing good work? It is my right. Not many put in the kind of long and hard hours I put behind my work. Plus, as people love and listen to me, it is also part of my strategy to popularize my schemes, using my name as a brand'.

As I have sought to address previously, where does the myth-maker Modi begin and where does he end as the high-tech geek enthusing over the marvels of technology in administration and in his personal communication with the public through social media such as Facebook and Twitter? Indeed, he has single-handedly led the country's politicians to tweeting, many of them for the first time. In physical terms, it is most reminiscent of the dhoti-clad Tamilian with caste marks on his forehead donning a western jacket and a necktie.

In his office as the country's prime minister, he might eventually catch on to the incongruity of his beliefs with trying to make India modern. One hopes for the country's good that the penny will drop sooner than later. It is, of course, by no means certain that he can rid himself of fantasies and, more importantly, succeed in getting the better of his mentors even if he did.

So the country must remain in suspense as Modi's own conflicts are resolved and his emancipation from the RSS is effected to an extent.

REFERENCES

Mahurkar, Uday. *Centrestage: Inside the Narendra Modi Model of Governance.* New Delhi: Random House India, 2014.

Marino, Andy. *Narendra Modi: A Political Biography.* New Delhi: HarperCollins *Publishers* India, 2014.

Mukhopadhyay, Nilanjan. *Narendra Modi: The Man, The Times.* Chennai: Tranquebar, 2013.

Nag, Kingshuk. *The NaMo Story: A Political Life.* New Delhi: Roli Books, 2013.

Ullekh NP. *War Room: The People, Tactics and Technology Behind Narendra Modi's 2014 Win.* New Delhi: Roli Books, 2015.

CAST OF CHARACTERS

Abe, Shinzo: Prime minister, Japan

Adityanath, Yogi: BJP member of Parliament

Advani, Lal Krishna: Senior BJP leader; former deputy prime minister, India

Ambedkar, Bhimrao Ramji: Independent India's first law minister, principal architect of the Constitution of India

Ansari, Hamid: Vice-president, India

Azad, Abul Kalam: Leader of the Indian independence movement; first education minister of independent India

Batra, Dinanath: Retired school teacher, RSS activist and convenor of Shiksha Bachao Andolan Samiti (Save Education Movement)

Bhagwat, Mohan: *Sarsanghchalak* (supreme leader) of the RSS

Bharti, Somnath: AAP leader; member of legislative assembly, Delhi

Bhushan, Prashant: Senior lawyer; former senior member of the AAP

Chauhan, Gajendra: Chairperson, Film and Television Institute of India, Pune; former actor, best known for his portrayal of Yudhisthira in the television series, *Mahabharata* (1988–90)

Chimanlal, Jashodaben: Wife of Indian prime minister, Narendra Modi

Chouhan, Shivraj Singh: BJP leader; chief minister, Madhya Pradesh

Chudasama, Bhupendrasinh: Education minister, Gujarat

Dikshit, Sheila: Senior Congress leader; former chief minister, Delhi

Fabius, Laurent: Foreign minister, France

Farooqui, Kamal: Member, Muslim Personal Law Board; former chairman, Delhi Minorities Commission

Gandhi, Indira: Former prime minister, India

Gandhi, Maneka: BJP leader; women and child development minister, Government of India; wife of Sanjay Gandhi

Gandhi, Mohandas Karamchand: Pre-eminent leader of India's independence movement

Gandhi, Rajiv: Former prime minister, India

Gandhi, Sanjay: Younger son of former Indian prime minister, Indira Gandhi

Gandhi, Sonia: President of the Congress Party and Rajiv Gandhi's widow

Gandhi, Varun: BJP member of Parliament, son of Sanjay and Maneka Gandhi

Godse, Nathuram Vinayak: Mahatma Gandhi's assassin

Hazare, Anna: Social activist, leader of the 'India Against Corruption' movement

Hedgewar, Keshav Baliram: Founder *Sarsanghchalak*, RSS

Irani, Smriti: Minister of human resource development, Government of India

Jaitley, Arun: Minister for finance, corporate affairs, information and broadcasting, Government of India

Jinnah, Mohammad Ali: The Quaid-i-Azam or 'Great Leader', founder and first governor-general of Pakistan

Kakodkar, Anil: Nuclear scientist, former chairman of the Atomic Energy Commission of India; former chairman, Board of Governors, Indian Institute of Technology, Mumbai

Kejriwal, Arvind: National convenor of the AAP; chief minister, Delhi

Khan, Liaquat Ali: First prime minister, Pakistan

Kumar, Nitish: Leader of the Janata Dal (United Party), chief minister of Bihar

Madhav, Ram: RSS ideologue; national general secretary, BJP

Mandal, Bindeshwari Prasad: Chairman, Mandal Commission (Second Backward Classes Commission)

Masani, Minoo: Former parliamentarian, leader of the erstwhile Swatantra Party

Mayawati: Leader of the Bahujan Samaj Party, four-time chief minister, Uttar Pradesh

Modi, Lalit: Businessman and cricket administrator, first chairman and commissioner, Indian Premier League (IPL)

Modi, Narendra: Prime minister, India

Mookerjee, Syama Prasad: Founder, Bharatiya Jana Sangh, forerunner to the BJP

Narayan, Jaya Prakash (JP): Activist in the Indian independence movement and social reformer. Led the opposition to Indira Gandhi during the Emergency years in the mid-1970s and called for 'total revolution' for her overthrow

Nariman, Fali S.: Constitutional jurist; senior advocate to the Supreme Court

Nehru, Jawaharlal: First prime minister, India

Netanyahu, Benjamin: Leader of the Likud party; prime minister, Israel

Obama, Barack: President of the United States of America

Owaisi, Asaduddin: President of the All India Majlis-e-Ittehad-ul Muslimeen, member of Parliament

Patel, Vallabhbhai: Leader of the Indian independence movement; first home minister, India

Rajagopalachari, Chakravarti: Leader of the Indian independence movement; last governor-general of India

Rao, P.V. Narasimha: Former prime minister, India

Rao, Y. Sudershan: Chairman, Indian Council of Historical Research

Rahmani, Maulana Muhammad Wali: Working general-secretary, All India Muslim Personal Law Board

Ribeiro, Julio: Former director-general of police, Punjab

Sardesai, Rajdeep: Senior journalist

Savarkar, Vinayak Damodar 'Veer': Indian nationalist and Hindutva ideologue

Scindia, Vasundhara Raje: BJP leader; chief minister, Rajasthan

Sen, Ashok Kumar: Barrister and former parliamentarian, law minister in Jawaharlal Nehru's cabinet

Shah, Amit: BJP president, credited with the efficient management of the BJP's election campaign in the national elections of 2014

Sharif, Nawaz: Prime minister, Pakistan

Shastri, Lal Bahadur: Second prime minister of India, led the country during the Indo–Pakistan War of 1965

Shevgaokar, Raghunath K.: Former director, Indian Institute of Technology, Delhi

Siddiqui, Shahid: Editor and publisher, *Nai Duniya*

Singh, Rajnath: Home minister, Government of India

Singh, Vishwanath Pratap: Former prime minister, India

el-Sisi, Abdel Fatah: Sixth president of Egypt, in office since June 2014

Swaraj, Sushma: External affairs minister, Government of India

Tarkunde, Vithal Mahadeo: Social reformer and co-founder (along with JP) of Citizens for Democracy and the People's Union for Civil Liberties

Thapar, Karan: Journalist and television personality

Togadia, Praveen: Leader of the Vishwa Hindu Parishad

Tomar, Jitender Singh: Former minister of law and justice in the Arvind Kejriwal-led Delhi government

Vajpayee, Atal Behari: First BJP prime minister of India

Vaz, Keith: British Labour Party politician and member of Parliament

Xi, Jinping: General Secretary of the Communist Party of China; president, People's Republic of China

Yadav, Lalu Prasad: President of Rashtriya Janata Dal; former chief minister, Bihar

Yadav, Yogendra: Former senior leader of the AAP, founding member of Swaraj Abhiyan and Jai Kisan Andolan

ACKNOWLEDGEMENTS

I would like to record my appreciation for the efficiency and speed with which Paranjoy Guha Thakurta and his team have handled my manuscript. I am, of course, responsible for any error that might have crept in.

I have already acknowledged borrowing from my political columns in *The Asian Age* and *The Tribune* to illustrate my arguments.

ABOUT THE AUTHOR

SURENDRA NIHAL SINGH, better known as S. Nihal Singh, started his career in journalism in 1954 as an apprentice sub-editor. Over six decades he has been editor of two of India's major newspapers, *The Statesman* and *The Indian Express*, and of Dubai's *Khaleej Times*. Nihal Singh was with *The Statesman* as editor in New Delhi and later chief editor in Kolkata.

He was given the International Editor of the Year award by the Atlas World Press Service in New York for his role during the Emergency. Apart from parliamentary and political reporting and analysis at various levels in India, Nihal Singh has served in various parts of the world as the newspaper's foreign correspondent. He was South-east Asia correspondent for five years based out of Singapore during the 1960's Vietnam War, Indonesia's confrontation with Malaysia and Singapore's short spell as one of the states of Malaysia. He was the first Indian newspaper correspondent to be posted in Pakistan after the 1965 war and opened a bureau in Moscow before returning to India and then moving again to London.

Among Nihal Singh's publications are his memoir *Ink in My Veins: A Life in Journalism, The Yogi and the Bear: A Study of Indo–Soviet Relations* and *The Rise and Fall of UNESCO*.